Cooking for Your Heart's Content

Cooking for Your Heart's Content

250 gourmet recipes to keep your heart healthy

Compiled by Dr. D. Wainwright Evans
and Meta A. M. Greenfield

PADDINGTON PRESS LTD
NEW YORK & LONDON

Acknowledgments

Thanks are due to the following for their help in preparing this book:

ICI PHARMACEUTICALS
THE FLOUR ADVISORY BUREAU – for recipes and preparing food for photography
MAZOLA CORN OIL LTD. – for recipes
KNORR LTD. – for recipes
BROWN AND POLSON LTD. – for recipes
DR. D. A. T. SOUTHGATE, THE DUNN NUTRITIONAL LABORATORY, CAMBRIDGE, ENGLAND
THE DIETITIANS GROUP AT ADDENBROOKE'S HOSPITAL, CAMBRIDGE, ENGLAND
VAN DEN BERGHS LTD. – for recipes
EDEN VALE LTD. – for recipes
DAVIS GELATINE LTD. – for recipes
LUCY HEDLEY – for recipes
J. BIBBY & SONS LTD. – for recipes
ALISON BOYD – for recipes
AMERICAN HEART ASSOCIATION – for recipes

Credits

Color photography by Clive Corless
Line drawings by Kate Simunek
Cooking pots, glass and oven dishes from a selection at
    Yvonne Peters, London and Selfridges, London
Fresh vegetables and salad foods from Robert Jackson, London

Library of Congress Cataloging in Publication Data
Main entry under title:

COOKING FOR YOUR HEART'S CONTENT

   Includes index.
1.   Cookery for cardiacs.   2.   Coronary heart disease – Prevention.   3.   Low-fat diet – Recipes.
4.   Low-cholesterol diet – Recipes.   I.   Evans, David Wainwright.   II.   Greenfield, Meta A. M.
RM221.C3H33   616.1'2'0654   77–5075
ISBN 0–448–23166–2

IN THE UNITED STATES
PADDINGTON PRESS LTD.
Distributed by
GROSSET & DUNLAP

IN CANADA
Distributed by
RANDOM HOUSE OF CANADA LTD.

Contents

Foreword

The following recipes offer a wide range of dishes – many of them in daily use – suitable for those who wish to minimize their risk of developing heart and circulatory disease. With these recipes it is simple to control fat and cholesterol intake without having to weigh every piece of food. They have been designed to make the food exciting and delicious and therefore should be attractive to all who wish to derive maximum enjoyment from their food, with a minimum risk for the future. The dishes will also appeal to those who have suffered a coronary attack, or who have arterial disease elsewhere, and have been advised to follow a diet designed to lower blood cholesterol levels.

Where excess weight is part of the problem, the total amount of food eaten must be carefully watched. Recipes most useful to dieters are clearly marked in the book and the chart on page 124 provides a quick guide to the more suitable foods. If you already follow a medically designed diet, keep to your own personal instructions.

The main aim of the British Heart Foundation is to finance and support research into the causes, prevention and treatment of diseases of the heart and circulation; ample reason for it to sponsor and highly recommend this book.

British Heart Foundation, London

Medical Introduction

Coronary heart disease, or ischaemic heart disease (IHD), is by far the biggest killer in our modern society. Among men over the age of thirty-five, deaths from this cause exceeded deaths from all forms of cancer combined. Behind this stark mortality lurks the specter of a restricted life for some of those whose hearts keep going after narrowing of the coronary arteries (the heart's own source of nutrition) has developed to a critical stage. All too often, this can mean unacceptable limitation of someone's life style just at the time of peak success and productivity.

While we are still far from a complete understanding of all the mechanisms involved in coronary heart disease and its various manifestations, there is already sufficient knowledge of major factors involved to give real hope that prevention of most premature coronary attacks may be feasible. Indeed, the recent downturn in the coronary death rate in the USA may reflect the success of public education efforts there, particularly with regard to smoking.[1]

Those seriously intent on minimizing their chances of falling victim to coronary heart disease, as well as to other diseases, will surely be non-smokers. They will also take advantage of any

1. Stamler, J., *Bulletin of the International Society of Cardiology*, ISC, Geneva, Summer 1975, page 5.

facilities for blood pressure checks at work or elsewhere. The third major factor is diet; appropriate action in this respect involves avoidance of obesity and reduction in the amount of fat consumed,[2] especially "saturated fat." This is fat in which the fatty acids have no double-bond linkages in their carbon chains. Fortunately it isn't necessary to understand chemistry in order to avoid such fats; it is almost enough to know that dairy fats and most others of animal origin are rich in them. This book is all about the ways and means of eating less of these fats.

In general terms, it is healthy to take regular, sensible exercise and the avoidance of stress is frequently advised. However, it is difficult to alter one's basic personality, standards or *raison d'être*, and for most responsible middle-aged people all that can reasonably be hoped for is the development of a certain "philosophy of maturity." This can usefully include a realistic appraisal of remaining ambitions and the abandonment of juvenile race-track attitudes when driving.

Other factors apart, a habitually high consumption of saturated fat is considered by some to be a *necessary* factor in the development of coronary heart disease.[3] It may explain the very high incidence of coronary disease amongst the bucolic Finns as contrasted with the low incidence among the highly stressed Japanese. The mechanism by which it favors arterial deposits and narrowing need not concern us here. Suffice it to say that the blood concentration of a substance called cholesterol appears to be an essential link and that fat of this type tends to increase it. To a lesser extent the amount of cholesterol itself in the diet is also involved. Vegetable and marine fats composed chiefly of unsaturated fats have either no effect on blood cholesterol or tend to reduce it.

A prudent diet, therefore, avoids excessive intake of food generally and involves reduction of saturated fat and cholesterol intake to an acceptable minimum. No more than a third of one's daily energy intake should be in the form of fat and at least half of this fat should be in the unsaturated form. In practice this means cutting out certain foods (especially dairy foods) altogether, while curtailing others and substituting alternatives. For example, one should forsake cream for ever, or at least feel deliciously guilty when, very exceptionally, falling to its temptation. Most cheeses and the obvious fat on meat should likewise be avoided. Butter and cooking fats of animal origin should be replaced by a suitable margarine or oil. Dried skim milk may be substituted for whole milk. Full details of the eating pattern are given in the next section, written by a dietitian long experienced in the practicalities of managing such wholesale changes within the family setting.

The recipes in this book were designed and collected to show that an interesting and varied diet can be enjoyed by those intent on keeping their blood cholesterol levels down. There is, incidentally, no virtue in deliberately consuming large quantities of unsaturated fat. This would surely lead to weight gain and be counterproductive (as is overconsumption of sugar, alcohol or any other food).

The degree of enthusiasm for these changes will vary with individual circumstances. People with identified high blood cholesterol problems are usually well motivated and should be under medical and dietetic care. It is hoped that these recipes will, if considered suitable by their advisers, help them to adhere to what might otherwise seem a monotonous diet. Fortunately, after a few months, there is often a striking change in food preferences so that fatty dishes are instinctively avoided. This greatly simplifies the problems of eating out, though these problems can be exaggerated. An occasional, truly exceptional, excess intake of saturated fat is of no material consequence. It is a low average consumption of fat over years or decades that really matters, for the influence of diet in the causation of coronary heart disease is probably very long term. For this reason it is hoped that at least some of the general population, and not just those known to be at special risk, may be influenced by the contents of this book to adopt and maintain a more prudent diet throughout adult life.

2. *Diet and Coronary Heart Disease*, HMSO, 1974.
3. Blackburn, H., *Progress in Cardiology (3)* (Ed. Yu and Goodwin), Lea and Febiger, Philadelphia, 1974.

DAVID WAINWRIGHT EVANS
Consultant Cardiologist
Addenbrooke's Hospital
Cambridge, England

The Good-hearted Diet

USEFUL TERMS

When starting a good-hearted diet, it helps to understand some of the terms you may meet. It is important to learn about fats so that you know which types are found in the different foods you eat.

Carbohydrates   These are found in starchy and sugary foods. They supply short-term energy for the body because they are digested quickly, especially sugar and glucose. Specifically they are:

Sugar: Sugar itself, glucose, syrup, molasses, jam and marmalade, sweet soft drinks.

Starches: Bread, cereals, flour, and products made with flour, potatoes, rice, corn, pasta.

Milk sugar: All milks, including skim milk, contain the carbohydrate called lactose.

Fruit sugar: The carbohydrate fructose is found in all fruits.

Cholesterol   This substance is normally present in the blood and is manufactured by the body. It is also obtained from foods. The levels of blood cholesterol vary widely in different parts of the world, depending mainly on local eating habits. A raised cholesterol level is implicated in coronary heart disease, plaques containing cholesterol being found in the walls of the arteries. Foods containing cholesterol come in five groups:

Cholesterol-free: All plants and vegetables and their products.

Low cholesterol: Skim milk and low-fat yogurt.

Medium cholesterol: White fish – cod, haddock, sole, plaice, whiting, etc. (including smoked haddock).
Oily fish – herrings, kippers, mackerel, tuna, salmon, sardines, lobster.
Meat – lean cuts of beef, lamb, pork, chicken, turkey, rabbit, ham, corned beef, lean canned meats.
Dairy products – milk, full-fat yogurt, cheese, except Cheddar.

Medium-high cholesterol: These contain two to four times as much cholesterol as food in the medium group: heart, beef or pig's liver, lamb's tongue, tripe, shrimps, cream, Cheddar cheese, whole egg.

High cholesterol: These contain over four times as much cholesterol as the medium group: egg yolk, brain, calf, chicken and lamb's liver, sweetbreads, fish roes.

Energy   The energy that food supplies is measured in units called *Calories*. Their full name is kilocalories. (When kilojoules replace them, the conversion factor will be $4 \cdot 2$ KJ = 1 Cal.) Protein, fat and carbohydrates all supply calories, but fat is the most concentrated source. It supplies two and a quarter times as much energy as the other two.

Fats   These give long-term energy because they take longer to be digested and absorbed into the system. They are found in foods as:

Visible obvious fats: Like lard, suet, cooking fat, oil, butter, margarine, fat on meat and cream.

Invisible fats: Like milk, fat in meat, cheese, oily fish. Small quantities are contained in cereals. Vegetables and fruit, apart from avocados and olives, contain a minimal amount of fat.

When chemically analyzed, fats contain, as part of their make-up, substances known as fatty acids. These come in three types:

Saturated fatty acid: These are found in foods of mainly animal origin. Over long periods eating too much food containing saturated fatty acids tends to increase blood cholesterol levels. These fats are found in: Cream, cheese, milk fat, butter, meat fat, cooking fat, dripping, lard, suet, coconut and palm oils, cocoa and chocolate; hard and soft margarines which are not specifically polyunsaturated.

Monounsaturated fatty acids: These neither raise nor lower the blood cholesterol levels. However, they do add to the total daily fat (and energy) intake. Foods containing them also have some saturated fatty acids as well. They are found in largest amounts in: olive oil, peanut oil, olives (black or green), avocados.

Polyunsaturated fatty acids: These tend to lower the

blood cholesterol level. They are usually liquid oils extracted from plant seeds such as safflower, sunflower, corn and soya bean. Polyunsaturated margarines are a convenient source of this type of fatty acid. It is important to remember that even the most highly polyunsaturated oil – safflower – is only 72 percent "poly," the rest being "mono" and saturated fat. The best soft margarines are about 50 percent "poly," the rest being "mono" and saturated.

Proteins These are the main body-building and repair foods. The best quality and most concentrated sources are found in meat, fish, cheese, milk, eggs, nuts and soya beans. The now fashionable textured vegetable proteins are extracted from soya beans and field beans. Then come the medium sources in quality and concentration: wheat flour, bread, wheat cereals, peas, broad beans, lentils, string and other dried beans. All protein-supplying foods are a mixture of protein and fat and/or carbohydrate.

Triglycerides These are also normally found in the blood. The body uses them for carrying fatty acids. Raised levels are usually associated with obesity and/or abnormal handling of carbohydrate by the body.

CHOOSING YOUR FOOD: HOW TO USE THE DIET

This section makes it simple for you to select the right foods for good-hearted eating.

Meat

Meat contains a great deal of invisible as well as visible fat, so meat portions must be small. Buy only lean cuts and beware of meat with too much fat marbled through it. Trim off all excess fat. If you always choose very carefully and trim before cooking, economical cuts can be used just as well as the more expensive ones. When buying ground beef, choose lean chuck steak and ask your butcher to grind it. If this is not possible, buy the best quality ground meat and strain off all the fat produced after browning the meat. Avoid fatty canned or prepared meats like luncheon meat, salami and sausages. Make certain that lamb, pork, ham or bacon really are lean. Pork, although it contains a little more fat than beef or lamb, contains a higher proportion of

polyunsaturated fat. Offal – kidneys, liver, etc. – is normally banned because it is high in cholesterol.

Poultry or White Meat

Chicken, turkey and rabbit contain less fat than other meats so can be eaten in larger portions. Beware of duck and goose, which are high in fat.

Fish

White fish, lobster and smoked haddock have a minimal fat content and can be eaten freely. Oily fish like herrings, mackerel, tuna and salmon, have as much fat as lean meat, but are low in saturated fat. Apart from lobster, all shellfish and fish roes are high in cholesterol, so should be avoided.

Dairy Produce

Avoid full-cream milk. Use skim milk, either as a powder made up into a liquid, or fresh skim milk, if it is available. If skim milk is not available at work or on vacation, a small amount of fresh milk with the cream siphoned off may be used. Omit cream, butter, full-fat yogurt, Cheddar and cream cheese of all types, including Camembert and Brie, because the fat content is very high. However, Dutch Edam and Gouda may occasionally be substituted for a small quantity of meat. Use cottage cheese freely as this is low in fat – the same applies to low-fat yogurt. Most plain well-known makes of ice cream contain only a little fat in small portions, so can be used 2–3 times a week, but avoid the richer types. Also avoid coffee creamers.

Eggs

Egg yolks are very high in cholesterol. On a low cholesterol diet, reduce these to one a week. Substitute liver for this one egg occasionally, because it is an invaluable source of concentrated iron and vitamins – especially important for children and women of child-bearing years. Liver is normally forbidden because of its high cholesterol content. Have as many egg whites as you want. They are allowed freely.

Fats and Oils

For cooking, use oils. The ones containing the greatest number of polyunsaturated fats are listed first: safflower, sunflower, soya bean, corn. Don't buy oils labeled anonymously "vegetable oil." Instead, choose one with the seed-oil content on the label. Although oil is used a great deal in these recipes, remember that your total fat intake should be rationed, especially if you are dieting. Avoid peanut, olive and coconut oils.

Margarine: use a brand which states it is "high in polyunsaturates." These are usually about 50 percent polyunsaturated. Other soft margarines fall into two groups, either about 30 percent or about 15 percent polyunsaturated, but it is not possible to state a named list as they can vary from season to season.

Sauces and Salad Dressings

Some of the ready-made brands may be suitable. Be sure to read the labeled contents carefully first because the oil used may vary depending on the variety available to the manufacturer.

Vegetables and Fruits

Use all vegetables and fruits freely, except for avocados and olives. Legumes are very good suppliers of protein and iron, economical, filling and low in fat. This group includes fresh, frozen, canned or dried peas, broad beans, lentils, string beans, baked beans, black eye and kidney beans. Dried peas, lentils and beans make good soups and help to fill out meat portions in stews and casseroles. A wide variety of these can be obtained from specialist grocers or health-food shops. Textured vegetable protein, made from soya and field beans, can also be used as there is a low saturated-fat content. Dieters should steer clear of vegetables that are high in calories like potatoes, corn, canned and processed peas and lentils.

Ready-to-Eat Foods

Most of these are unsuitable. Read package labels carefully to check if they contain unsaturated fats. Remember that labels have to list ingredients in order of quantity. The ingredient present in largest quantity is always listed first. Some plain biscuits like water biscuits or matzos and some crispbreads can be included. If you are on a prescribed diet, check first with your dietitian. Bought cakes, pastries and "take-out" foods, unless known to be cooked with the correct margarine or oil, are not suitable.

Sugar, Desserts and Alcohol

Sugar, jam, marmalade, syrup and sugary soft drinks, as well as alcohol, should all be used in moderation. This group should be more severely restricted if blood triglycerides are high or if you are overweight.

Advice for Dieters

Many of the extra calories in the recipes found in this book come from carbohydrate foods like potatoes, pasta, rice and flour, or from the special cooking oil or margarine. It is easy to reduce the calorie value. Either use oil or margarine merely to grease the pan before browning meat, or use a non-stick pan. This will save 264 calories per 1 fl. oz of oil, and 226 calories per 1 oz of margarine. Omit the oil from French dressing and make a dieter's version from vinegar and seasonings, or the juice of a fresh lemon, adding a crushed clove of garlic or a pinch of mustard for extra bite. Remember, you are allowed a certain amount of oil or margarine each day, which can be accounted for in the recipes.

Thickenings, like cornstarch or flour, can easily be left out of stews, and other dishes like vegetable soups, making a calorie saving of 100 per 1 oz. If rice, pasta and potato are included in the recipe, serve only your allowed portion from the day's carbohydrate ration. If the calories for a main course are about 200–250 per serving, this is suitable for dieters. A helpful list of food portions for dieters can be found in the appendix on page 125. Also the chart on page 124 gives a speedy guide to choosing the right foods to help you lose weight.

Advice for Diabetics and Those Restricting Carbohydrates

Some people may be on a "carbohydrate exchange" type of restricted diet. This will include many diabetics. These are different from calorie-restricted diets as only the carbohydrates are being counted while varying protein and fat content of foods will alter the calories considerably. Eating portions are worked out in terms of 10 g carbohydrates (C). These portions can be interchanged to vary daily eating. Adapt the recipes by omitting or counting the thickening in main course dishes, soups and so on, so they have the appropriate amount of carbohydrates from potatoes, rice and pasta to conform with your individual allowance. Although you will have your own portion list, there is also one on page 125 which will help you to use these recipes. Before adapting these recipes, it is wise to consult your dietitian.

Advice for People with Stomach Disorders

People suffering from stomach or duodenal ulcers, or from hiatus hernia, can easily adapt this diet to their needs. General advice is to eat small meals regularly; do not go a long time without food; avoid all fried food; use oil or special margarine in cookery for stews, soups, and French dressings. Increase your skim milk, low-fat yogurt and cottage cheese allowance if you need more milky foods. Bran, often advised for diverticular disease or constipation, can be used with this diet. Anyone wishing to increase "roughage" in daily eating, can add a tablespoon of bran to their breakfast cereal each morning.

Vegetarian Diets

It is relatively easy for vegetarians to follow a good-hearted diet, especially if the basis of their diet is legumes like peas, dried beans, lentils, etc. or textured vegetable protein. But it is more of a problem if egg and cheese are the mainstay of the diet. However, many cheeses are not higher in cholesterol than meat, so can be eaten instead of it. Try to keep the egg intake down to 3–4 a week, and try to introduce more of the legumes as a suitable alternative protein source.

EATING OUT

This can present problems for any dieter. However, an occasional fling does little harm, especially if you make up afterwards by taking special care. A suitable meal can usually be chosen from a restaurant menu. Fruit juices, melon, grapefruit, other fruit cocktails and consommé soups are all free of fat and cholesterol. Choose plain meat and fish dishes, avoiding rich concoctions. Don't choose dishes with rich sauces. Vegetables, salads without dressing, potatoes, rice, etc. are fine, but avoid sautéed, roast or French fried potatoes where possible. Don't choose rich, creamy sweet dishes. Instead go for fruit, ice creams or sherberts, which are a safer bet.

If you are on an especially rigid diet and visiting friends or staying in a hotel, remember to say what you can eat. Don't just reel off a long list of banned food – it is very off-putting to a cook or hotel staff.

PREPARING AND COOKING YOUR FOOD

It is important to remove all visible fats before cooking – this applies to poultry as well as red meat. Minimize the fat content in stocks, soups and stews or casseroles by skimming the fat off occasionally during cooking. Allow the dish to cool after cooking, then remove any fat after it has solidified – it is easier this way and you can get rid of the fat more efficiently. *Always* substitute oil and polyunsaturated margarine for other fats when cooking. Many of your own recipes can easily be adapted. Simply use polyunsaturated oils and fats instead of butter or lard as in the original recipe.

Use cooking methods which remove fat, like baking, boiling, broiling, roasting and stewing. When roasting meat, place it on a rack, then put this in the roasting pan. Add a little oil, marinade, stock, or tomato juice to keep it moist – not meat fat or dripping. Then cover with foil. The foil helps to keep the meat moist without basting, and reduces shrinkage in roast meat, especially if a small piece is being cooked. An alternative way is to place the meat on a rack in a covered roasting pan – this works out more economically in the long run than buying foil. Always pour off all the fat from the pan after cooking and make the gravy from the drippings of the meat. A double-lipped gravy boat with a deep funnel at one end to pour the stock from under any surface fat is a great help. Cook roast vegetables like onions and potatoes in oil in separate pans.

Do not overheat cooking oil. It reaches much higher temperatures before smoking than other fats so food added at this temperature burns on the outside before it is cooked on the inside. Do not add food to oil which is not hot enough, otherwise it absorbs too much fat and tastes greasy and indigestible. Test the temperature by frying a cube of bread first. This should turn nicely brown and crisp in 30 seconds. Whenever possible use shallow frying methods with oil. Always use fresh oil each time. An efficient non-stick frying pan helps, because it needs little or no oil. After cooking, excess fat should be removed by draining the food on paper towels. Use oil when making French dressing, mayonnaise, marinades, sauces, and cakes and biscuits, as well as pastry. It does not take long to use up your daily oil allowance – be careful it is not exceeded.

Aim to adapt the family meals to the needs of the diet, so that double cooking is only necessary occasionally, otherwise the diet becomes a chore, not merely the modification of a way of life. Remember that growing children need more vitamins and minerals in proportion to their size than adults do. Some foods not allowed on this diet should be included for children, like unskimmed milk, egg yolks and liver, which are good sources of iron and vitamins A, B and D.

Using up excess egg yolks need not be a problem. Some can be used to make egg custards or egg-yolk mayonnaise for special occasions. If you really are stuck with the extra yolks, they can be used outside the kitchen. Egg yolk is a popular beauty aid. It makes a good hair conditioner. Mix with a little lemon juice, rub into the hair after washing and rinse with luke-warm water.

Cottage cheese can be used successfully for cooking as a topping for pizzas, in soups and for snack dishes. It is easy to pep up the taste if you are using it on its own by adding chopped fresh herbs, seasonings and mustards.

Use your ingredients like a painter's palette. Experiment to invent your own recipes or embellish existing ones in your own way. Good cooking does not necessarily mean that everything should be smothered in cream, egg yolks and butter. The new cooking style in France, pioneered by Chef Michel Guerard, shuns these old *cordon bleu* favorites. Instead he uses gently cooked vegetables puréed to a cream, concentrating on cutting down the unnecessary calories. His foods are often cooked quickly and simply to bring out maximum flavor without suffocating in fat. Experimental cooking of this type is fun to do if there is a bit of spare time, and well worthwhile if you can add your own individual touches to everyday eating.

META A. M. GREENFIELD, S.R.D.
Senior Dietitian
Addenbrooke's Hospital
Cambridge, England

Breakfasts

Breakfast should be a light meal for the good-hearted diet. Concentrate on fresh fruit and cereals, not the traditional cooked breakfast. If you crave for bacon and eggs, it can be worth using the weekly allowance of one whole egg for a special Sunday-morning treat. Cook the egg in your favorite way, perhaps boiled, or fried in oil with broiled bacon and tomatoes. In cold weather, eat cooked fish for a warm start to the day. Have your usual morning tea or coffee, but with skim milk and preferably without sugar. Add a daily tablespoonful of bran to breakfast cereal to pep up the digestive system and keep it running smoothly. Apart from home-made fruit juices, bought varieties are also good for breakfasts, but always check the ingredients on the label first.

Breakfast kedgeree

½ *cup rice*
¾ *cup cooked smoked haddock*
2 tablespoons cooking oil
seasoning
1 hard-boiled egg white, chopped
fresh chopped parsley

386 calories per serving
Cook rice, flake fish. Place oil in pan, add seasoning, egg white, rice and flaked fish. Heat thoroughly. Mix in the parsley, reserving some for garnish. *Serves 2.*

Muesli

8 parts flaked or rolled oats
1 part wheat germ
1 part chopped dates
1 part dried apple
1 part dried apricot
1 part white raisins
1 part skim milk powder
1 part soft brown sugar (optional)
1–2 parts bran

Use a metal container with a tight lid to store the muesli, which can be made in bulk. The oats are the basis. Choose any or all of the other ingredients to suit your taste, and combine everything together in the container. Eat either with skim milk or, often more refreshingly, with unsweetened orange juice.

Breakfast baked fish

1 lb white fish fillets or smoked haddock
½ cup skim milk
½ teaspoon polyunsaturated margarine
seasoning
small bay leaf (optional)

Suitable for dieters: 131 calories per serving
Place fish and skim milk in baking dish. Dot with margarine. Season well, add bay leaf, and bake in a covered dish for 20 minutes, using a moderate oven, 375°F, 190°C. *Serves 4.*

Breakfast lemon drink

1 lemon
1 teaspoon clear honey or use artificial
  sweetener
1 cup hot water

With honey: 47 calories. Suitable for dieters with sweetener: minimum calories
Squeeze lemon into glass. Add honey, then stir with teaspoon and pour hot water on top. This healthy drink makes a refreshing start first thing in the morning. As an added bonus, the lemon is said to help keep the complexion clear.

Home-made tomato juice

2 lb firm ripe tomatoes
4 tablespoons water
salt

Suitable for dieters: 21 calories per serving
Wash tomatoes, cut out stems, remove any soft spots and chop roughly. Add water to saucepan and simmer gently until soft, about 5–10 minutes. Put through fine sieve. Return to pan, add salt and heat to boiling point. Place in covered jar or bottle and keep in refrigerator. Serve with Worcestershire sauce. With an electric juicer, the fresh juice can be extracted from the tomatoes without cooking. *Serves 6.*

Soups And Starters

Fresh home-made soup is one of the best beginnings to any meal. Soup does not need to be laced with cream to be good. Fresh vegetables gently cooked with a subtle home-made stock, then puréed until they are smooth and creamy textured, taste delicious. Bouillon cubes are great helpers if you are short of time. Home-made stocks from bones and root vegetables are economical. If you are using fresh marrow bones, first brown them in a hot oven for about an hour. Cook them gently in a heavy stew pot with plenty of water, vegetables and herbs, to make the stock. Always reheat a stock pot daily for 20–30 minutes to keep it fresh. Full-bodied soups make a good snack meal. Always skim excess fat from any soup before serving. When choosing starters, select lighter recipes or small salads (*see* Salad section).

Celery soup

1 bunch celery
2 beef or chicken bouillon cubes
1½ cups hot water
2 tablespoons skim milk powder

Suitable for dieters: 37 calories per serving
Wash and scrub celery and chop coarsely. Dissolve bouillon cubes in hot water. Add celery and cook till tender, 30–40 minutes. Purée or beat till smooth. Return to pan and stir in skim milk powder and reheat. *Serves 2.*

Zucchini and tomato soup

2 chicken bouillon cubes
½ cup hot water
1½ cups tomato juice
1 lb zucchini, peeled, cored and diced
1 chopped onion or 2 teaspoons onion flakes
salt, pepper
few drops sweetener (optional)

Suitable for dieters: 55 calories per serving
Dissolve bouillon cubes in hot water; add the rest of the ingredients except salt, pepper and sweetener, and bring to the boil. Cover pan and simmer gently until zucchini is cooked, about 20 minutes. Purée and return to the pan; season with salt, pepper and liquid sweetener, and reheat. *Serves 2–3.*

Gazpacho (illustrated opposite)

1 clove garlic
1 large onion, chopped
2 lb tomatoes, skinned
2 tablespoons cooking oil
1 cup beef stock
4 tablespoons vinegar
salt, pepper
pinch cayenne
1 teaspoon paprika
4 tablespoons chopped parsley
Garnish:
   green pepper, finely chopped
   cucumber, finely chopped

Suitable for dieters: 72 calories per serving
Blend all ingredients until smooth in an electric blender. Chill soup thoroughly; add a few ice cubes just before serving. Place vegetables for garnish in separate small bowls, so guests can help themselves.   Serves 4.

Kipper pâté (illustrated opposite)

2 boned kippers
½ cup white sauce:
   2 tablespoons flour
   ¾ oz polyunsaturated margarine
   ½ cup skim milk
1 oz polyunsaturated margarine
2 tablespoons lemon juice
cayenne
¼ teaspoon ground mace

Suitable for dieters: 175 calories per serving
Place kippers head down in a wide-mouthed jar and pour boiling water over them till covered. Leave to stand for 5 minutes. Pour off water, remove all skin and bones from kippers and allow to cool. Beat kippers till smooth and then blend in sauce, margarine, skim milk, lemon juice, and season with cayenne and mace. Store in refrigerator. Serve with toast or use a sandwich filling.   Serves 4.

Mushrooms with herbs (illustrated opposite)

8 oz button mushrooms
4 tablespoons lemon juice
4 tablespoons oil
1 teaspoon milled coriander seeds
2 bay leaves
seasoning, freshly milled pepper

Suitable for dieters: 74 calories per serving
Wash mushrooms. Trim stalks. Cut into thick slices. Place in dish with a squeeze of fresh lemon. Heat oil and coriander in heavy pan. Add mushrooms, bay leaves and seasoning. Cover pan and cook slowly for 5 minutes. Place in serving dish with bay leaves and pan juices. Add a further sprinkling of lemon juice and oil. Serve cold or hot.   Serves 4.
   Suitable for dieters, if you use oil from day's ration.

Borscht (illustrated opposite)

4 medium-sized raw beets
2 beef bouillon cubes
4 cups water
1 onion, studded with cloves
1 level teaspoon caraway seeds
1 cup shredded vegetables: leek, cabbage,
  celery
4 tablespoons oil
salt, pepper
pinch nutmeg
½ cup low-fat natural yogurt

118 calories per serving
Peel and slice 3 beets; put into saucepan with bouillon cubes, water, onion studded with cloves, and caraway seeds. Simmer gently for 1 hour or until color has run from beets into stock. Sauté shredded vegetables and finely grated fourth beet in heated oil for 10–15 minutes. Strain stock, pressing out all juice from beets; return to pan. Add shredded vegetables and simmer until these are cooked. Season to taste and add nutmeg. Purée in blender until smooth, or leave as a chunky soup. Stir in yogurt; reheat but do not boil. Garnish with a swirl of yogurt.   *Serves 4–6.*

Chilled cucumber and yogurt soup (illustrated opposite)

2 large cucumbers
2 cloves garlic, crushed
1 teaspoon finely chopped mint
½ teaspoon grated lemon rind
2 tablespoons lemon juice
salt, pinch black pepper
2 tablespoons oil
1 cup low-fat natural yogurt
3 chicken bouillon cubes
2 cups hot water

Suitable for dieters: 41 calories per serving
Peel and seed cucumbers; then grate them. Beat garlic, mint, lemon rind and juice, salt, pepper and oil into yogurt until smooth. Add cucumber. Dissolve bouillon cubes in hot water, add to yogurt mixture and chill thoroughly before serving. Garnish with thin slices of cucumber and chopped mint or parsley.   *Serves 6.*

Country vegetable soup (illustrated opposite)

3–4 cups chopped root vegetables: potatoes,
  carrots, turnips, celery, etc. including leeks
  and onions
1 oz polyunsaturated margarine
4 cups water or meat stock
optional: 1 medium can baked beans or ½ cup
  dried beans, soaked overnight

130 calories per serving
Toss chopped root vegetables in margarine. Add water or stock and beans. Bring to the boil and cook gently for 45 minutes, if using baked beans, or 2 hours, if using dried beans. Serve as a delightful chunky soup or blend for smooth thick soup. Garnish with parsley.   *Serves 6.*

Cream of carrot soup

1 lb carrots
2 medium potatoes
1 small onion
4 tablespoons corn oil
2 mixed herb bouillon cubes, dissolved in 3
  cups hot water
½ cup skim milk
chopped parsley

163 calories per serving
Peel vegetables and chop. Heat oil in large frying pan and sauté vegetables for 2–3 minutes. Add stock, bring to boil and simmer gently for 1 hour. Rub through sieve or blend, add milk and reheat without boiling. Garnish with freshly chopped parsley.   *Serves 4.*

Leek and potato soup

1 lb leeks
2 onions
1 lb potatoes
2 oz polyunsaturated margarine
½ cup skim milk
4 cups stock or use water and 2 chicken
  bouillon cubes
salt and pepper
chopped parsley to garnish

157 calories per serving
Trim the leeks, slice lengthwise through to the center and wash thoroughly in cold water. Shred the leeks finely. Peel and chop onions. Melt margarine in a large frying pan, add leeks and chopped onions and fry gently for about 10 minutes – do not brown. Add peeled and diced potatoes and cook for a further 5 minutes before adding the hot stock and seasoning. Bring to the boil and simmer for 30–40 minutes. Purée the soup, return to pan, add skim milk, reheat and serve hot, garnished with chopped parsley. This may be serve chilled.   *Serves 6.*

Cucumber soup

1 small cucumber
1 small onion
2 cups chicken stock or use 1 chicken
  bouillon cube to 2 cups water
pepper and salt to taste
pinch onion powder or onion salt
1 teaspoon lemon juice
2 level teaspoons cornstarch

Suitable for dieters: 30 calories per serving
Peel and thinly slice cucumber and onion. Bring stock to boil. Add sliced cucumber and onion and simmer gently about 5 minutes or until tender. Add seasonings and lemon juice. Mix cornstarch smoothly with a little cold water, stir into soup and boil for 3 minutes, stirring constantly. For a smooth soup, put this through a sieve or blender. Serve hot or cold.   *Serves 2–3.*

Spinach soup

1 lb fresh spinach or block of frozen spinach
½ oz polyunsaturated margarine
1 onion, finely chopped
2–4 cups chicken or beef stock, using
* bouillon cube*

Suitable for dieters: 57 calories per serving
Cook onion in margarine. Add fresh spinach. Cook in covered saucepan for 3 minutes until leaves look droopy. Add stock. Cook for further 10 minutes. Purée in blender. Add seasoning and serve. (If using frozen spinach, add it when cooked to onion. Top up with stock and cook 8–10 minutes.) *Serves 4.*

Variation: *Watercress soup.* Use 2 bunches of washed watercress instead of spinach and follow same method for recipe.

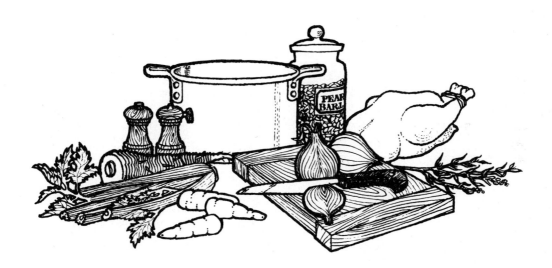

Chicken broth

1 chicken carcass and giblets
4–6 cups water
1 onion
1 carrot
1 clove garlic (optional)
stalk of celery or other chopped vegetables in
* season*
salt, pepper
fresh chopped chives to garnish

Suitable for dieters: 10 calories per serving
Cook chicken, vegetables and water gently for at least 2 hours to reduce. Strain into bowl. Leave in refrigerator. Remove fat when cool. Heat up stock for broth, adding chopped chives.
Serves 6.

If stock has turned into a good jelly when cold, this can be served as jellied consommé on warm summer days.

Mulligatawny soup

4 tablespoons cooking oil
4 oz onions, chopped
4 tablespoons flour
3 cups stock
2 teaspoons curry powder
$\frac{1}{4}$ teaspoon salt
4 oz carrots, sliced
1 teaspoon lemon juice
2 teaspoons tomato purée
1 bay leaf
2 tablespoons long-grain rice

252 calories per serving
Heat oil and sauté onions without browning for 5 minutes. Add flour stirring well and cook gently without browning for 1 minute. Gradually add stock, stirring all the time until the mixture thickens. Add curry powder, salt, carrots, lemon juice, tomato purée and bay leaf. Simmer for 30–45 minutes or until vegetables are tender, then pass through a strainer or remove bay leaf and use an electric blender. Add rice and simmer for about 15 minutes or until the rice is tender.   *Serves 4.*

Sherried onion consommé (illustrated on page 65)

4 medium onions, sliced
1 cup dry sherry
2 cloves garlic, crushed
black pepper
sprig parsley
2 beef bouillon cubes, dissolved in 3 cups
    boiling water
2 tablespoons fresh orange juice
garnish: onion rings, orange peel

75 calories per serving
Place onions, sherry, garlic, pepper, parsley and stock in saucepan. Bring to boil simmer gently for 30 minutes or until onions are very soft. Strain liquid into bowl, add orange juice. To serve: garnish with onion rings or thin strips of orange peel.   *Serves 6.*
  Suitable for dieters if sherry is omitted.

Onion soup

$1\frac{1}{2}$ lb onions, thinly sliced
$1\frac{1}{2}$ oz polyunsaturated margarine
2 tablespoons cooking oil
salt
$\frac{3}{4}$ teaspoon sugar
$\frac{1}{4}$ cup flour
$6\frac{1}{2}$ cups brown beef stock

Suitable for dieters: 79 calories per serving
Cook onions slowly in oil and margarine with salt and sugar. Add flour, and stir well. Add stock and simmer for 40 minutes. Serve with slices of French bread.   *Serves 8.*

Calorie-counters' soup

5 cups water or stock
*3 cups cubed or thinly sliced vegetables in
    season (carrots, celery, leeks, mushrooms,
    onions, turnips, rutabagas, string beans,
    peas – not potatoes)*
chopped parsley

Suitable for dieters: 22 calories per serving
Prepare vegetables and cook for 30 minutes in
liquid. Serve, garnished with chopped parsley.
Serves 6.

Cream of mushroom soup

1 tablespoon finely chopped onion
2 oz polyunsaturated margarine
8 oz mushrooms
¼ cup flour
2 cups stock
2 cups skim milk
seasoning

223 calories per serving
Cook the onion till soft in margarine. Add
chopped mushrooms and sauté for 4–5 minutes.
Add the flour and stir well, not browning. Add
stock and milk gradually. Bring to the boil, stirring all the time. Season and cook for 5
minutes.   *Serves 4–5.*

Cock-a-leekie soup

1 chicken, about 3 lb
salt
6 peppercorns
6 leeks

Suitable for dieters if used as a main course:
131 calories per serving
Put the chicken and giblets in a large saucepan.
Add salt and peppercorns and bring to the boil.
Remove any film from the surface and cook for 1½
hours with the lid on. Cut off the roots and trim
coarse green from the leeks to within 2 in of the
white stems. Slice lengthways through to the
center and wash thoroughly in cold water. Chop
into 1-in pieces. Skim the soup again and add
leeks. Simmer 30 minutes more. Remove chicken
and giblets from the soup. Remove skin and
bones; set aside best breast meat for another
recipe. Cut remaining meat into small pieces; add
to soup; check seasoning. Garnish with chopped
parsley.   *Serves 6.*

Cream of celery soup

1 oz polyunsaturated margarine
2 tablespoons flour
2 cups skim milk
seasoning
2 bunches celery
2 cups stock or water

195 calories per serving
Make a thin white sauce with margarine, flour and milk. Season well. Cook the scrubbed and chopped celery in stock or water until tender. Purée and combine with the white sauce, stirring well. *Serves 4–6.*

Cream of celery and artichoke soup

1 lb Jerusalem artichokes
1 bunch celery
½ oz polyunsaturated margarine
5 cups stock or water
seasoning

Suitable for dieters: 33 calories per serving
Peel and slice artichokes; scrub and chop celery. Melt margarine and toss vegetables in this for 3–5 minutes. Add stock and seasoning, and cook 30–40 minutes. Purée. Serve garnished with chopped parsley. *Serves 6.*

Cream of chicken soup

1 tablespoon onion, minced or finely
  chopped
2 oz polyunsaturated margarine
¼ cup flour
3½ cups chicken stock
1 cup skim milk
seasoning
½ cup cooked chicken, chopped

165 calories per serving
Cook onion till soft in margarine. Blend in flour, but do not brown. Gradually stir in stock and skim milk. Bring to the boil and simmer for 5 minutes. Add seasoning and cooked chicken. Simmer for a further 5 minutes and serve garnished with chopped parsley. *Serves 6.*

Lucy's soup

2 onions, thinly sliced
2 large potatoes, thinly sliced
1 cup water
4 oz cottage cheese
sea salt
freshly milled pepper
1 cup skim milk

132 calories per serving
Add onions, potatoes and cottage cheese to water in saucepan. Season and boil for 10 minutes until vegetables are cooked. Blend till smooth in blender, or put through sieve. Add milk. Reheat gently, stirring. Serve, garnished with shredded cabbage or carrot. *Serves 4.*

Suitable for slimmers, if used as a main course.

Scotch broth

$\frac{1}{2}$–1 lb neck of lamb
4 cups water
2 tablespoons barley
salt, pepper
bouquet garni
$\frac{1}{4}$ cup turnip, diced
1 leek, sliced
2 carrots, diced
1 small carrot, grated

218 calories per serving
Wash meat. Trim off fat, and put meat into a large saucepan. Add water, salt and barley (washed); bring to the boil. Add pepper, bouquet garni and vegetables. Cook for $1\frac{1}{2}$–2 hours, or until the meat is tender. Half an hour before serving add the grated carrot. When cooked, skim off excess fat and remove bouquet garni. Garnish with chopped parsley. This is a substantial soup which can be used as a main course. *Serves 4.*

Tomato soup

1 lb canned or fresh tomatoes
2$\frac{1}{2}$ cups stock and tomato liquid, mixed
piece of carrot and celery
1 small onion
$\frac{1}{2}$ oz lean bacon
$\frac{1}{2}$ oz polyunsaturated margarine
bay leaf, mace
1 tablespoon cornstarch
$\frac{1}{2}$ cup skim milk

98 calories per serving
Strain liquid from tomatoes and add to stock to make $1\frac{1}{4}$ pt. Sauté chopped onion, celery, carrot and bacon in margarine. Add tomatoes and reduce heat for 3–5 minutes. Add stock, bay leaf and mace; simmer for 1 hour. Strain and purée tomatoes but not other vegetables. Thicken with cornstarch dissolved in cold skim milk. Serve with strips of thin toast. *Serves 4.*

Julienne soup

1 carrot
1 medium onion
¼ turnip
1 stalk celery
½ oz polyunsaturated margarine
seasoning
4 cups chicken stock

Suitable for dieters: 29 calories per serving
Clean and peel vegetables. Cut into matchstick shapes. Melt margarine in small pan. Gently sauté vegetables for 5 minutes without browning. Drain on paper towels to remove fat. Add to hot chicken stock. Simmer for 15 minutes, skimming if necessary.   *Serves 4.*

Hunter's soup

1 oz polyunsaturated margarine
4 oz raw lean ham or bacon, sliced
1 onion, sliced
1 carrot, sliced
1 or 2 stalks celery
4 cups chicken stock
1 oz cooked chicken or rabbit, chopped
seasoning, bouquet garni

204 calories per serving
Melt margarine, add ham and chopped vegetables and soften. Add stock and cooked meat, seasoning and bouquet garni. Simmer gently for 1 hour. Skim any excess fat off top of soup before serving, garnish with chopped fresh herbs. A substantial soup good for using as a main course.   *Serves 4.*

Suitable for dieters if used as a main course.

Lentil soup

6 oz lentils
1 large onion, chopped
1 oz polyunsaturated margarine
4 cups meat stock or water and 2 bouillon
  cubes
1 tablespoon cornstarch
1 cup skim milk
chopped parsley

150 calories per serving
Wash lentils. Soak overnight. Drain. Toss onion and lentils gently in melted margarine. Add stock and seasoning. Cover, bring to the boil and simmer, skimming occasionally, for 2 hours or until lentils are soft. Sieve and return to pan. Mix cornstarch with a little milk. Add to soup with rest of milk. Bring to the boil, stirring. Serve garnished with parsley.   *Serves 6.*

Scandinavian herrings (illustrated on page 64)

4 small rolled pickled herrings
1 red apple, sliced
½ red pepper, sliced
1 medium onion, cut into rings
½ cup special mayonnaise (page 68)

170 calories per serving
Toss apple, pepper and onion in mayonnaise.
Place in serving dish with the herrings.   *Serves 4.*

Smoky fish starter

1 lb cooked smoked fish
½ cup tomato juice
½ teaspoon Worcestershire sauce
½ teaspoon grated horseradish
½ teaspoon lemon juice
½ teaspoon vinegar
4 tablespoons chopped parsley

Suitable for dieters: 118 calories per serving
Flake the fish. Mix with other ingredients and
serve on shredded lettuce.   *Serves 4.*

Easy eggs

6 eggs
4 oz mushrooms
½ cup skim milk
½ cup cooked chicken
salt, pepper, paprika
chopped parsley

Suitable for dieters: 81 calories per serving
Hard boil eggs; cool and shell. Cut in half lengthwise and remove yolks. Wash mushrooms and slice thinly into saucepan. Add milk and stew slowly for 15 minutes with pinch of salt. Slice chicken and add to mushrooms and liquid. Place in blender and blend until smooth. Tip mixture into a bowl. Add seasoning and mix well. Heap into egg whites. Garnish with a little paprika and serve cold on strips of toast or bread.   *Serves 4.*

Haddock relish

1 oz polyunsaturated margarine
8 oz fresh or canned tomatoes
2 tablespoons flour
salt and pepper
pinch of dry mustard
1 cup skim milk
¼–¾ cup flaked cooked smoked haddock
2 teaspoons parsley

Suitable for dieters: 150 calories per serving
Melt margarine in a saucepan. Stir in tomatoes (sliced and skinned if fresh). Season and add a pinch of dry mustard. Stew gently until tender, then sprinkle in flour and cook for a minute or two. Add seasoning and skim milk gradually, stirring all the time, and cook for a few minutes. Add smoked haddock and heat through. Add chopped parsley and serve on hot toast.
Serves 4.

Marinated herrings

2 small fresh herrings, filleted
½ cup vinegar and water mixed
¼ teaspoon salt
1 blade mace
2 cloves
6 peppercorns

Suitable for dieters: 200 calories per serving
Wash and clean herrings. Roll up, beginning at the tail end. Secure with a toothpick. Place in a small pie pan with seasoning; cover with vinegar and water. Bake in a moderate oven, 325°F, 160°C, for ½–¾ hour.   *Serves 2.*

Rabbit and turkey terrine

1 lb rabbit
thyme
4 peppercorns
2 bay leaves
2 cups stock or water
1 onion, sliced
½–1 clove garlic (optional)
salt and pepper
¾ cup cooked turkey
⅓ cup white sauce:
1½ tablespoon flour
¾ oz polyunsaturated margarine
⅓ cup skim milk

Suitable for dieters as a snack meal: 137 calories per serving
Cook rabbit in stock with thyme, peppercorns, bay leaves and sliced onion until tender. Leave to cool. Grind the rabbit flesh, turkey and onion and beat well with a little of the stock, the white sauce, salt, pepper and crushed garlic. Cover and keep in the refrigerator. Serve with toasted brown bread. *Serves 8.*

Anchovies in a basket

2 cooked beets
1 large can anchovies
2 hard-boiled egg whites
2 small dill pickles
seasoning
vinegar
2 tablespoons chopped fresh herbs

87 calories per serving
Halve beets. Scoop out centers to make baskets. Soak in vinegar. Thinly slice anchovies, egg whites and dill pickles. Mix. Season with salt, pepper and vinegar. Add herbs. Drain beets. Fill with anchovy mixture. Chill before serving. *Serves 4.*

Grapefruit starter

2 grapefruits
2 oz polyunsaturated margarine
4 tablespoons brown sugar

52 calories per serving
Cut grapefruits in half, using a serrated knife. Loosen segments so grapefruits can be served in their skins and are easy to eat with a teaspoon. Divide margarine into 4, and place a pat on each grapefruit half. Sprinkle with sugar. Broil under Medium heat for about 6 minutes. Serve hot. *Serves 4.*

Hot Main Dishes

Nourishing stew, simple roast or grill – whatever your favorite hot dish, the most important thing to remember is that it should contain as little fat as possible. Bread or paper towels are both useful for skimming fat off casseroles. Portions of dishes should not be too large. Make the most of white fish dishes because they contain useful protein. It is well worth experimenting with different herbs and seasonings to alter the flavor of homely recipes. These can often taste a little bland when cooked for diet purposes, so the seasonings and herbs are much needed to pep up the flavor. For additional information see the Introduction, page 9.

Rabbit casserole

1 rabbit
seasoned flour
$\frac{1}{3}$ cup cooking oil
4 onions, sliced
parsley, thyme
salt, pepper
1 cup stock or mixed stock and red wine or
    cider

373 calories per serving
Joint rabbit and roll in seasoned flour. Brown joints quickly in hot oil. Cover with sliced onion and sprinkle with parsley, thyme, salt and pepper. Add stock and simmer in a tightly covered saucepan or casserole over a low heat, or in the oven at 325°F, 160°C, for 45 minutes to 1 hour. Skim off surplus fat before serving. *Serves 4.*

Rabbit pie

$\frac{3}{4}$ cup flour
3 oz polyunsaturated margarine
pinch salt
$\frac{1}{2}$ teaspoon baking powder
1 rabbit, in serving pieces
seasoned flour
$\frac{1}{4}$ cup cooking oil
$\frac{1}{2}$ cup stock
mixed herbs
grated rind of 1 lemon

674 calories per serving
Make pie pastry by combining flour, margarine, salt and baking powder, adding water to mix. Dip rabbit joints in seasoned flour. Brown in hot oil and place in a pie pan with stock, mixed herbs and grated lemon rind. Roll out pastry to just larger than the pie pan. Cut off a strip of pastry, moisten edges of pan and place strip of pastry round. Moisten strip and place remaining pastry over pie. Trim off excess pastry. Make a hole in the top. Cook for 20 minutes at 400°F, 200°C, then for 1$\frac{1}{2}$ hours at 250°F, 120°C. *Serves 4–6.*

British fish pie

4–6 oz flaked cooked white fish
2 hard-boiled egg whites, sliced
2 tomatoes, sliced
1 cup skim milk to make savory parsley
   sauce
salt and pepper

Suitable for dieters: 158 calories per serving
Place layers of sauce, flaked fish, tomato and egg in a fireproof dish. Finish with a layer of sauce. Brown in the oven for 30 minutes, 375°F, 190°C. Use sliced boiled potato in place of the parsley sauce as a variation. *Serves 2.*

Russian fish pie

¾ cup flour
3 oz polyunsaturated margarine
salt
½ teaspoon baking powder
8 oz smoked haddock
½ cup white sauce:
   ½ oz polyunsaturated margarine
   1 tablespoon flour
   ½ cup skim milk
1 teaspoon chopped parsley
dash lemon juice
salt, pepper

466 calories per serving
Make pie pastry by combining flour, margarine, salt and baking powder, adding water to mix. Cut fish into small pieces and mix with sauce, parsley and lemon juice. Season with salt and pepper. Roll pastry out into a square. Trim and place mixture in center. Brush edges of pastry with skim milk, fold corners to center and seal. Decorate with pastry leaves, place on baking sheet and bake in a hot oven, 425°F, 220°C, for 40–45 minutes. (Cooked fish may be used.) *Serves 4.*

Salmon croquettes

1 tablespoon finely chopped onion
4 oz polyunsaturated margarine
4 tablespoons flour
½ cup skim milk
8-oz can pink salmon or tuna, well drained
and flaked
pepper
8 tablespoons fine dry breadcrumbs

604 calories per serving
Sauté onion in half margarine until just tender Stir in flour and cook for 1 minute, stirring constantly. Blend in milk and cook, stirring, over medium heat until thick. Cool slightly. Stir in salmon and pepper. Add half breadcrumbs; mix thoroughly. Shape into 6 patties or logs and roll in remaining crumbs. Sauté in rest of margarine until evenly browned on all sides. *Serves 3.*

Fish skillets

1 lb fish fillets or steaks
¾ cup cooking oil
1 onion, chopped
⅓ cup chopped green pepper (optional)
¼ cup chopped parsley
2 medium tomatoes, cut in pieces or 8-oz can
    tomatoes
½ cup water or tomato juice
½ teaspoon salt, pepper
½ teaspoon basil or oregano

Suitable for dieters: 212 calories per serving
If fish is frozen, thaw it enough to separate pieces. Heat oil in frying pan. Add onion, green pepper and parsley and cook until onion is golden, about 5 minutes. Add tomatoes, water or tomato juice, and seasoning; cook until tomatoes are soft. Add fish, cover and cook gently, about 10 minutes or until fish is done.   *Serves 4.*

Baked fish in chives

Four 5–6-oz fish steaks
2 oz polyunsaturated margarine
2 tablespoons lemon juice
2 tablespoons chopped chives
salt, pepper
chopped parsley
lemon slices

377 calories per serving
Brush fish with half-melted margarine and sprinkle with lemon juice. Arrange in a greased shallow baking dish and cover with foil. Bake for 30 minutes at 350°F, 180°C, until the fish flakes easily when tested with a fork. Combine remaining margarine with chopped chives and seasoning and heat slightly. Arrange fish on serving platter and pour over warm herb mixture. Garnish with parsley and slices of lemon.   *Serves 4.*

Broiled fish steaks

1 lb fish steaks
2 teaspoons cooking oil per portion
salt, pepper, paprika
lemon juice
chopped parsley

Suitable for dieters: 163 calories per serving
Arrange fish in preheated oiled baking pan. Add 2 teaspoons oil for each serving of fish. Sprinkle with salt, pepper and paprika. Bake at 500°F, 260°C, for about 15 minutes or until fish flakes easily when tested with a fork. Do not turn unless fish is very thick. Sprinkle with lemon juice and chopped parsley before serving.   *Serves 4.*

Oven-fried fish fillets

1 lb fish fillets or small whole fish
½ cup dry breadcrumbs
6 tablespoons French dressing
(2 parts cooking oil to 1 part vinegar/lemon/
lime juice)

Suitable for dieters: 273 calories per serving
If frozen fish is used, thaw it enough to separate pieces. Dip fish into well-seasoned French dressing, then into breadcrumbs. Arrange on an oiled baking sheet. Pour any remaining French dressing over fish. Bake at 500°F, 260°C, for 10–12 minutes, or until the fish flakes easily when tested with a fork. Serve with tossed mixed salad. *Serves 4.*

Fish cakes

½ cup cooked white fish
½ cup cold cooked potato
salt, pepper
1 teaspoon chopped parsley
juice of 1 lemon
flour for coating
cooking oil

366 calories per serving
Flake fish, mash potato, mix together and season with salt, pepper, chopped parsley and lemon juice. Divide into equal portions. Shape into flat cakes with a little flour. Fry in oil slowly until golden brown. Drain on paper towels. Serve garnished with lemon and parsley.   *Serves 2.*

Mushroom cod

1 lb cod fillet
4 oz button mushrooms, sliced
1 small onion, chopped
2 oz polyunsaturated margarine
skim milk
2 tablespoons flour
salt, pepper
chopped parsley
aluminum foil

Suitable for dieters: 256 calories per serving
Skin fish; cut into 3 even-sized pieces; wash and dry. Season. Place in center of greased foil on a baking sheet. Heat half margarine and cook mushrooms and onion gently until soft but not brown. Spoon onto fish. (Reserve any margarine in pan for sauce.) Fold over sides of foil, overlapping edges to form a loose parcel. Bake at 375°F, 190°C, for 35–40 minutes. Open foil and drain juices into a measuring cup; make up to 1 cup with skim milk. Melt rest of margarine, blend in flour and cook for 1 minute without browning. Add liquid, stirring. Bring to boil. Season. Pour sauce over fish and sprinkle with parsley.   *Serves 3.*

Paupiettes of plaice (illustrated opposite)

1 large plaice (or lemon sole), filleted
little polyunsaturated margarine
4 oz mushrooms, thinly sliced
1 small onion, chopped
1 tomato, skinned and chopped
2 tablespoons cooking oil
salt, pepper
medium package frozen peas
chopped parsley

Suitable for dieters: 177 calories per serving
Lightly grease baking foil, lay in 2 fillets in the shape of fish. Put half mushrooms down center of fish. Sauté onion and tomato in oil until soft. Add to mushroom filling. Cover with remaining fillets and rest of mushrooms. Season. Fold over foil so that juices cannot escape; place in fireproof dish and bake at 300°F, 150°C, for 15–20 minutes. Open up foil carefully. Arrange edges to hold juices. Surround with cooked peas and garnish with finely chopped parsley. *Serves 4.*

Spanish cod (illustrated opposite)

1½ lb cod fillet
2 thick slices brown bread
1½ oz polyunsaturated margarine
1 clove garlic, crushed
juice and grated rind of 1 orange
salt, pepper
orange slices
watercress

367 calories per serving
Make bread into crumbs. Melt margarine in frying pan. Add crumbs, garlic and orange rind. Shake and stir until crumbs have absorbed all margarine. Place cod fillet in greased fireproof dish, season well with salt and pepper and cover with breadcrumbs and orange juice. Bake uncovered at 375°F, 190°C, for 20–30 minutes. Garnish with orange slices and watercress. Watercress salad and new potatoes are good accompaniments. *Serves 3.*

American fish pie (illustrated opposite)

10 oz cooked fish
1 cup white sauce:
    1½ tablespoons flour
    ¾ oz polyunsaturated margarine
    1 cup skim milk
1 teaspoon chopped parsley
squeeze lemon juice
salt, pepper
2–3 tomatoes
1 lb cooked potatoes
1 oz polyunsaturated margarine
skim milk

322 calories per serving
Remove all skin and bones from fish and mix with sauce. Add parsley, lemon juice and seasonings. Skin and slice tomatoes. Mash potatoes. Melt margarine in a saucepan; add potatoes, seasonings and skim milk; beat until soft and creamy. Put a layer of potato in a greased pie pan and fill the dish with alternate layers of fish mixture and sliced tomatoes. Top with the rest of the potato and bake at 350°F, 180°C, until brown on top and well heated through, about ½ hour. *Serves 4.*

Kebabs (illustrated opposite)

Marinade:
  4 tablespoons cooking oil
  4 tablespoons dry sherry
  2 tablespoons vinegar
  salt, freshly ground pepper
  2 medium onions, sliced

12–14 oz lean leg lamb, cubed
12 button mushrooms
slices green or red pepper, 12 small onions
cubes of pineapple, 4 tomatoes, halved

275 calories per serving
Place meat in a bowl and cover with marinade. Leave at least 1 hour – overnight if possible. Remove meat and press on 4 skewers alternating with mushrooms, green pepper, onion, cubes of pineapple and finishing each end with $\frac{1}{2}$ tomato. Broil under hot broiler, turning occasionally and brushing with marinade. Serve on a bed of white or brown rice.   *Serves 4.*

Goulash (illustrated opposite)

8 tablespoons cooking oil
1$\frac{1}{2}$ lb lean chuck steak
1 lb onions, sliced
4 tablespoons flour, 6 peppercorns
1 teaspoon capers, chopped
1 teaspoon parsley, chopped
1$\frac{1}{2}$ teaspoons paprika, 1 teaspoon salt
2 bay leaves, 1 teaspoon marjoram
$\frac{1}{2}$ cup sherry (optional)
$\frac{1}{2}$ cup stock
$\frac{3}{4}$ cup spaghetti or noodles

485 calories per serving
Cut steak into 1-in cubes and lightly brown in half the oil. Remove from frying pan. Sauté onions without browning for 5 minutes. Return steak to pan, stir in flour, bay leaves, peppercorns, capers, parsley, paprika, salt and marjoram. Add stock and sherry (or substitute equal quantity of stock), stirring well, and bring to boil, cover and simmer gently for 1$\frac{1}{2}$–2 hours or until the steak is tender. Drain well. Remove the bay leaves from the goulash and serve on a dish with the spaghetti or noodles as a border. Garnish with chopped chives or parsley and freshly ground pepper.   *Serves 6.*

Burgundy pot roast (illustrated opposite)

6 tablespoons cooking oil
2$\frac{1}{2}$ lb lean beef top round
$\frac{1}{3}$ cup minced onion
2 cups sliced celery
1 clove garlic, finely chopped
$\frac{3}{4}$ cup stock
$\frac{1}{3}$ cup tomato purée
$\frac{1}{2}$ cup red wine

Suitable for dieters: 366 calories per serving
Heat oil in a large heavy pot. Add beef and cook over medium heat, turning to brown on all sides. Drain off all oil. Add remaining ingredients and bring to boil; cover and continue cooking in moderate oven, 350°F, 180°C, until tender, 2$\frac{1}{2}$–3 hours. Serve with boiled potatoes and fresh vegetables in season. The vegetables can be added to the casserole just before serving. Remove the meat to a separate plate for carving. Extra sauce may be served in a gravy boat.   *Serves 8.*

Sukiyaki

1½ lb lean rump steak
1 cup stock
⅓ cup soy sauce
½ teaspoon seasoning salt
4 tablespoons cooking oil
2 cups diagonally sliced celery
1½ medium onions, sliced
12 oz mushrooms, sliced
12 oz fresh spinach, cleaned

317 calories per serving

Slice meat, cutting across grain, into thin diagonal strips 3 × 1 in. Combine stock, soy sauce and seasoning salt. Heat 2 tablespoons of the oil in a large heavy pot; add half meat and brown, turning frequently. Add half soy sauce mixture, then push meat to one side of the pan. Add half of all the vegetables, except spinach, keeping each vegetable separate; cook, turning often, 3–4 minutes. Add half the spinach and cook 1–2 minutes longer. Place on serving dish. Serve at once with rice and sauce from pan. Cook remaining ingredients using the remaining 2 tablespoons of oil. Serve in the same way.   *Serves 6.*

Chili con carne

2 tablespoons cooking oil
1 lb ground lean beef
1 lb onions, chopped
2 cloves garlic, crushed
12 oz tomatoes, skinned and chopped
½–1 tablespoons chili powder, to taste
1 green pepper, sliced
½ cup red kidney beans, soaked
¼ teaspoon salt
½ cup water
4 tablespoons flour

305 calories per serving

Heat oil and sauté ground beef and onions together with garlic until lightly browned. Add tomatoes, chili powder, green pepper, red kidney beans, salt and three tablespoons of the water. Cover and simmer gently for approximately 45 minutes, stirring occasionally. Mix flour with the remaining water, pour into mixture and cook for 5 minutes. Serve with whole boiled potatoes. *Serves 4.*

Beef patties

1 lb ground lean beef
1 teaspoon lemon juice
grated rind of 1 medium lemon
¼ cup fine dry breadcrumbs
1 teaspoon salt
¼ teaspoon sage
¼ teaspoon ginger
½ cup beef stock or 1 bouillon cube, dissolved in
   ½ cup boiling water

Suitable for dieters: 241 calories per serving

Mix meat, lemon juice and rind, crumbs and seasoning together thoroughly. Add stock, mix thoroughly and let stand 15 minutes. Form into 4 meat patties, 3 in in diameter and ¾ in thick. Brush pan with oil. Pre-heat for about 3 minutes. Place patties in pan. Cook 7–8 minutes on each side. Mixture may also be made into a meat loaf if desired. *Serves 4.*

Fried rice with beef

8 oz lean rump steak, cut into 1-in squares
1 tablespoon soy sauce
¾ cup long-grain rice
½ cup cooking oil
8 oz onions, chopped
¼ medium cabbage, shredded
2 stalks celery, chopped
salt and pepper

429 calories per serving
Marinade steak in soy sauce for 20 minutes. Cook rice in plenty of boiling salted water until tender, approximately 15–20 minutes, rinse and drain. Heat 2 tablespoons of the oil and gently sauté rice for 5 minutes, remove and keep warm. Heat remaining oil and sauté onions, cabbage and celery with salt and pepper for 5 minutes. Add steak to vegetables and cook together for 5 minutes. Return rice to pan and cook all the ingredients together for 5 minutes, stirring continuously. Serve with chopped parsley, tomato and green pepper salad. *Serves 4.*

Country skillet

4 tablespoons cooking oil
1 lb ground beef
8 oz onions, sliced
8 oz carrots, grated
4 oz mushrooms, sliced
2 tablespoons flour
salt, pepper
1 cup stock, boiling
⅓ cup uncooked oatmeal, lightly toasted

442 calories per serving
Heat oil and gently sauté ground beef, onions, mushrooms and carrots until lightly browned. Stir in flour, cook for 2 minutes. Add salt, pepper and stock, cover and simmer for 15 minutes. Stir in oatmeal, cover and simmer for 20 minutes, stirring occasionally. Serve with triangular pieces of toast, green peas and boiled potatoes.
Serves 4.

Three marinades for steaks

1. ½ cup French dressing

2. ¼ cup cooking oil
   ¼ cup vinegar
   1 teaspoon salt
   ½ teaspoon Worcestershire sauce
   ½ teaspoon garlic salt

3. 1 cup red wine
   1 large onion, sliced
   1 teaspoon ground ginger
   1 lemon, sliced very thinly
   1 tablespoon salt
   12 peppercorns

These three marinades help to add extra flavoring to steaks. In each case, mix the various ingredients first. Pour over the meat. Let the meat then stand, covered, in a refrigerator overnight. Bring meat to room temperature before cooking and drain on paper towels. Then either broil or pan fry. These quantities are sufficient for 4–6 servings of meat.

Oxtail stew

1 lb oxtail
2 tablespoons flour
1 tablespoon cooking oil
2 cups stock, salt
1 onion, 1 carrot
¼ cup turnip
mixed herbs or bouquet garni
blade of mace, 6 peppercorns

292 calories per serving
Trim all excess fat from oxtail pieces. Blanch in boiling water. Dry oxtail pieces on paper towels, dip in seasoned flour and brown in oil. Add stock and salt; bring to the boil and skim. Add vegetables, herbs, peppercorns and mace, and cook for 3–4 hours, stirring occasionally. A pressure cooker is a great help with this dish. *Serves 4.*

Stuffed beef heart

1 lb beef heart
2 tablespoons breadcrumbs
1 onion, chopped
salt, pepper
sage or parsley, thyme
2 cups thin brown gravy

Suitable for dieters: 180 calories per serving
Trim the heart, cutting away sinews and fat to make a pocket. Wash well in cold salted water and dry. Season inside and out with pepper and salt. Mix breadcrumbs, onions, seasonings and herbs and use to stuff heart. Stitch or tie securely. Place in a deep casserole and pour over brown gravy. Cover and bake at 350°F, 180°C, until tender, about 3–4 hours. A pressure cooker considerably speeds up the cooking time. Some bought stuffing mixes are suitable, but check ingredients list.
Use only occasionally. *Serves 4.*

French country beef stew

5 medium onions, sliced
4 tablespoons cooking oil
2 lb top round or chuck steak
3 tablespoons flour
pinch marjoram and thyme
pinch salt and pepper
½ cup dry red wine with ¼ cup meat stock or
    ¾ cup meat stock
8 oz mushrooms, sliced
tomato juice may be added for extra flavor

Suitable for dieters, if wine omitted: 293 calories per serving
Cut beef into 1-in cubes. Brown onions in oil in heavy frying pan. Remove onions to another dish. Roll meat in flour mixed with seasonings. Sauté beef in remaining oil until brown. Add wine and stock (or use all stock). Stir mixture well. Simmer as slowly as possible for 1½–2 hours. Add more wine and stock (2 parts wine to 1 part stock) as necessary to keep beef barely covered. Return onions to pan after meat mixture has cooked 1½–2 hours. Add mushrooms and stir. Cook 30 minutes longer. Add more wine and stock if necessary – sauce should be thick and dark. Serve with boiled new potatoes and peas. *Serves 8.*

Carbonnade of lamb

1 lb lean leg of lamb
1 tablespoon seasoned flour
1 oz polyunsaturated margarine
4 tablespoons cooking oil
1 lb onions, thinly sliced
1 clove garlic, crushed
2 cups brown ale
salt, pepper
2 tablespoons sherry (optional)

514 calories per serving
Cut lamb into 1-in cubes and coat with seasoned flour. Melt margarine with oil and add onions and garlic. Cover and sauté gently for 15–20 minutes, stirring occasionally, until onions are completely soft. Remove onions, place in casserole. Sauté lamb in remaining fat until brown on all sides. Add to onions with brown ale and a little salt and pepper. Cover and cook in a moderate oven, 350°F, 180°C, for 1½ hours. Before serving, check seasoning and add sherry. Serve with creamed or new potatoes and tossed green salad. *Serves 4.*

Lamb provençale

1 lb lean leg of lamb, cooked
2 oz polyunsaturated margarine
2 tablespoons cooking oil
2 medium onions, chopped
14-oz can tomatoes
1 tablespoon tomato purée
1 cup dry white wine
4 oz mushrooms, sliced
1 large green pepper, seeded and sliced
salt, freshly ground black pepper

329 calories per serving
Cut lamb into ½-in cubes. Melt margarine with oil and add onions. Sauté gently for about 10–15 minutes until soft but not brown. Stir in tomatoes, tomato purée and wine. Bring to the boil and add lamb. Simmer, covered, for 25 minutes. Add mushrooms and green pepper and cook for a further 15 minutes, stirring occasionally. Season with salt and pepper. Serve with creamed potatoes and string beans.   *Serves 6.*

Lamb à l'orange

1 small onion, very finely chopped
2 tablespoons cooking oil
1 large orange
2 tablespoons redcurrant jelly
1 cup stock, skimmed
½ teaspoon dry mustard
½ teaspoon sugar
pinch cayenne pepper
2 tablespoons cornstarch
12 oz lean, cooked leg or shoulder of lamb

Suitable for dieters: 1183 calories
Sauté onion gently in oil until soft but not brown. Grate orange rind; cut three fine slices from orange. Trim pith and reserve for garnish. Squeeze juice from remainder of orange and add to onion with rind, redcurrant jelly and stock. Bring to boil, reduce heat and cook, stirring, for 5 minutes. Blend mustard, sugar, pepper and cornstarch together with 4 tablespoons cold water and stir into orange sauce. Slice lamb, add to sauce and bring to boil. Reduce heat and simmer for 15 minutes. Serve garnished with reserved orange slices. *Serves 4.*

Ceylon curry

1 lb lean cooked lamb
2 medium onions, finely chopped
2 tablespoons cooking oil
1 oz polyunsaturated margarine
1 tablespoon curry powder
1 teaspoon curry paste
2 tablespoons tomato purée
½ teaspoon each ginger, cinnamon, salt
1 bay leaf
½ cup stock, skimmed
4 oz mushrooms, chopped
3 small zucchini, 4 tomatoes
6 tablespoons sweet pickle or chutney

467 calories per serving
Cut lamb into 1-in cubes. Sauté onion in oil and margarine until soft and golden brown. Add curry powder and curry paste and cook for 10 minutes more, stirring occasionally. Add tomato purée, ginger, cinnamon, salt and bay leaf and mix well. Stir in stock. Add mushrooms, zucchini (sliced), tomatoes (chopped) and pickle. Add lamb and bring to boil, stirring constantly. Cover and simmer for 45 minutes, stirring occasionally. Serve with pilau rice, i.e. rice flavored with spices and cooked in stock. *Serves 4.*

Lamb chops Maria

4 tablespoons cooking oil
3 lean lamb chops
1 cup sweet white wine
1 clove garlic, crushed
3 tablespoons cornstarch
juice of half a lemon
½ teaspoon rosemary
1 bay leaf
salt and pepper
lemon wedges

376 calories per serving
Heat oil and lightly brown lamb chops on both sides. Add white wine, crushed garlic, lemon juice, rosemary, bay leaf, salt and pepper. Cover and simmer for 40 minutes. Place chops on serving dish and keep warm. Strain liquid, add cornstarch and return to heat, stirring continuously until sauce thickens. Pour sauce over the chops. Garnish with wedges of lemon. Serve with carrots and potatoes. *Serves 3.*

Somerset lamb with rice

⅓ cup cooking oil
8 oz onions, chopped 1½ lb lean leg of lamb
6 tablespoons flour
1 teaspoon salt
¼ teaspoon pepper
2 cups cider
8 oz tomatoes, skinned and quartered
1 small package frozen peas
¾ cup long-grain rice
1 tablespoon chopped parsley

596 calories per serving
Cut lamb into 1-in cubes. Heat oil and sauté onions and lamb for about 5 minutes or until lightly browned. Add flour, salt and pepper and cook gently for 1 minute. Gradually add cider, stirring constantly until mixture thickens. Cover and simmer gently for approximately 45 minutes. Then add tomatoes and peas. Cover and simmer again until meat is tender. Meanwhile cook rice in plenty of boiling water until only just tender. Rinse in boiling water, drain and dry well. Serve lamb mixture sprinkled with parsley and bordered with rice.   *Serves 6.*

Irish stew

1 middle neck or breast of lamb
1 lb potatoes
4 oz onions
1 cup water or stock
salt, pepper

Suitable for dieters: 270 calories per serving
Trim fat off the meat and cut into small pieces. Put into a casserole or stew pot and cover with hot water or stock. Add salt and bring to boil. Peel and slice onions. Wash and peel potatoes and cut one or two in half. Add onions and 1–2 sliced potatoes to the meat, season with pepper and simmer for 1½–2 hours. About 40 minutes before serving, add rest of the potatoes whole or cut in two.

N.B. The remains of cooked lamb makes excellent Irish stew but should be thoroughly reheated only after the onions and potatoes are tender. Serve dieters with ration of potatoes from the stew.   *Serves 4.*

Lamb and string beans

1 lb lean lamb – middle neck or breast
2 tablespoons oil
2 tablespoons flour
2 cups stock or water
2½ oz string beans
onion, sliced
carrot, turnip, celery, diced

423 calories per serving
Wash string beans and soak overnight. Trim fat off meat and cut into medium-sized pieces. Heat oil in a stew pot and brown the lamb quickly on both sides; lift out onto a plate. Sauté onion till a golden-brown color. Add stock or water, salt, pepper, meat and other vegetables including the string beans. Bring to the boil and simmer for 2 hours or cook in the oven, 325°F, 160°C. Baked beans may be used instead of string beans. *Serves 4.*

Lemon ginger chops

4 lean chops of lamb
Marinade:
  ½ cup cooking oil
  grated rind of 1 lemon
4 tablespoons lemon juice
2 tablespoons brown sugar
  1½ teaspoons ground ginger
  salt and pepper

373 calories per serving
Mix marinade ingredients together. Place chops in shallow dish and pour marinade over them. Leave for 2–3 hours, turning occasionally. Remove chops and place under hot broiler. Cook for 15 minutes, turning chops occasionally and basting them with marinade. Serve with baked potatoes and mixed salad. *Serves 4.*

Shepherd's pie

8 oz cold cooked meat or cooked ground beef
1 onion, chopped
½ tablespoon oil
½ tablespoon flour
½ cup stock or water, pepper and salt,
  mixed herbs (optional) to cover
1 lb cooked potatoes
2 tablespoons skim milk
pepper and salt

Suitable for dieters: 235 calories per serving
Heat oil in frying pan and sauté onion, add flour and cook till brown. Add stock slowly, stirring well. Remove skin and gristle from cooked meat and chop or grind it. Add meat to gravy and season well. Pour into a pie dish. Mash potatoes, adding milk, pepper and salt, beating till smooth. Put potatoes evenly over the meat, decorate with a fork or knife and bake at 350°F, 180°C, for 18–20 minutes. Other vegetables may be added, e.g. cooked peas, baked beans, cooked celery, skinned tomatoes. *Serves 4.*

Lamb hot-pot

1 lb stewing lamb, i.e. lean best end neck
1 lb potatoes
4 oz onions
4 oz carrots
4 oz celery
salt, pepper, parsley

275 calories per serving
Trim excess fat from meat. Peel and slice potatoes, slice onions and carrots, chop celery. Place a layer of potatoes in a casserole, season with salt and pepper. Add a layer of meat and a sprinkling of vegetables. Repeat layers, finishing with potatoes. Add water almost to cover. Cook, covered, over a very low heat for 2½ hours till the meat is tender. Skim off excess fat and serve sprinkled with parsley. *Serves 4.*

Roast veal with wine sauce

3–5 lb piece of roasting veal
1 tablespoon cooking oil
1 onion, chopped
1 carrot, grated
1 stalk celery, grated
½ cup dry white wine
½ teaspoon salt
freshly ground pepper
½ teaspoon basil
¼ teaspoon garlic powder
½ teaspoon sugar

434 calories per serving
Heat oven to 450°F, 230°C. Place meat in oil in roasting pan. Bake for 20 minutes, turning frequently to brown all over. Spread vegetables over top of meat. Cover pan with foil. Reduce heat to 300°F, 150°C. Bake for 2 hours, or until meat is tender. Remove meat from pan and set aside to cool. Place meat juices in bowl and refrigerate. As soon as the juice is cool, skim fat off. Rub meat juices with vegetables through strainer and place in large pan. Add wine and seasonings to meat juice mixture. Slice veal thinly and add to mixture. Heat through and serve.   *Serves 6–8.*

Braised veal with herbs

2 lb veal cutlets
4 tablespoons cooking oil
2 medium onions, cut in rings
1 clove garlic (optional)
¼ cup water
4 tablespoons lemon juice
½ teaspoon crushed oregano
1 teaspoon salt
4 tablespoons chopped parsley

239 calories per serving
Cut veal into serving pieces. Heat oil in large frying pan. Add veal; cook until brown on both sides. Remove from pan, add onions and garlic and cook until onions are tender. Remove garlic. Add veal, water, lemon juice, oregano and salt. Cover and simmer over low heat, turning meat occasionally until it is tender, about 30 minutes. Add extra water if necessary. Serve with chopped parsley.   *Serves 6.*

Breaded veal steaks

Four 4-oz veal steaks, cubed
4 tablespoons fine dry breadcrumbs
salt, pepper
2 oz polyunsaturated margarine

240 calories per serving
Dredge steak in crumbs seasoned with salt and pepper. Sauté slowly in margarine until browned on one side. Turn and brown on other side, allowing about 5–6 minutes per steak. Serve with new potatoes and fresh salad in season.   *Serves 4.*

Veal scallopini

1 small clove garlic, quartered
4 tablespoons cooking oil
4 small veal cutlets
2 tablespoons flour
½ teaspoon salt
few grains freshly milled pepper
few grains nutmeg
1 small onion, thinly sliced
½ cup Sauternes or other dry wine (or part tomato juice)
4-oz can mushrooms, drained
½ teaspoon paprika
2 tablespoons chopped parsley

392 calories per serving
Sauté garlic in oil over low heat for 5 minutes. Remove garlic and discard. Brown meat on both sides in oil over medium flame. Mix flour, salt, pepper and nutmeg; sprinkle over browned meat. Cover with onion and wine. Cover pan; simmer about 20 minutes turning meat several times. If liquid in pan renders down, add a little more wine. Add sliced mushrooms, cover and continue cooking 8–10 minutes more. Serve on warm platter with sauce over meat. Sprinkle with paprika and parsley. Serve with plain boiled rice and green salad. *Serves 4.*

1 lb thinly sliced veal steak cut into 3-in squares may be used instead of veal cutlets.

Casserole of veal

1 lb fillet of veal, cubed
1 onion, sliced
2 oz chopped mushrooms
salt and pepper, chopped parsley
bouquet garni, 2 tablespoons lemon juice
2 cups fat-free stock or water
2–4 level tablespoons cornstarch
skim milk

Suitable for dieters: 163 calories per serving
Remove any fat from meat. Put meat, vegetables, flavorings and stock in casserole and cover. Simmer until meat is tender. Thicken with a little cornstarch blended with skim milk. Sprinkle with chopped parsley. Serve with boiled rice and zucchini. *Serves 4.*

Veal Pilaf

⅓ cup cooking oil
1 lb onions, chopped
1 lb veal, diced
1 clove garlic, crushed
¼ cup almonds, split
¼ cup raisins
2 tablespoons crystallized ginger, finely chopped
1 teaspoon salt, ¼ teaspoon pepper, bay leaf
2 cups stock
1 cup long-grain rice

766 calories per serving
Heat oil and sauté onions and veal gently, without browning, for 5 minutes. Add garlic, almonds, raisins, crystallized ginger, salt, pepper, bay leaf and stock. Bring to the boil, then cover and simmer for about 45 minutes to 1 hour, or until veal is cooked. Stir in rice, cover and continue cooking until rice is tender, about 20 minutes. Garnish with chopped parsley. Serve with tomato and onion salad. *Serves 4.*

Pork chops with plum sauce

⅓ cup cooking oil
4 lean pork chops

Plum sauce:
  1 lb plums
  ½ cup water
  2 tablespoons flour
  3 tablespoons sugar
  ¼ teaspoon rosemary
  salt and pepper

811 calories per serving
Stone plums and simmer in water until soft, then sieve. Heat oil and lightly brown each chop on both sides, reduce heat and cook for approximately 7 minutes on both sides. Drain well on paper towels and keep warm. Stir flour into remaining oil in pan, cook for 1 minute. Gradually add plum purée, stirring all the time. Add sugar, rosemary, salt and pepper and simmer for 3 minutes, serve with the chops. Serve with fried tomatoes, creamed potatoes and French beans. *Serves 4.*

Pork and cider casserole (illustrated on page 64)

⅓ cup cooking oil
4 lean pork chops
2 tablespoons flour
2 cups cider
salt and pepper
8 oz apples, peeled and sliced
8 oz onions, sliced
8 oz tomatoes, skinned and sliced
or ½ cup cranberries

872 Calories per serving
Heat oil and cook chops until lightly browned on both sides, then remove from pan. Mix flour with oil and cook for 1 minute. Pour in cider gradually and stir continuously until sauce thickens. Add pork chops, salt, pepper, apples, onions and tomatoes (or cranberries) to sauce, cover and simmer gently for 40 minutes. Serve with broccoli spears and creamed potatoes.   *Serves 4.*

Apricot-stuffed pork chops

4 lean pork chops
4 tablespoons cooking oil

Apricot stuffing:
  4 oz dried apricots soaked overnight
  ⅓ cup white breadcrumbs
  2 teaspoons sage
  2 teaspoons parsley, chopped
  salt and pepper

475 calories per serving
Slit each chop lengthwise from edge of meat to bone. Make stuffing by straining and chopping apricots and mixing them with other ingredients and then pressing together. Divide stuffing into four and fill each chop with mixture. Heat oil and lightly brown chops on both sides. Cover and cook gently for approximately 15 minutes. Drain well on paper towels. Garnish with parsley. Serve with creamed potatoes and spiced red cabbage.   *Serves 4.*

Pork and mushrooms

2 tablespoons cooking oil
1 teaspoon salt
1 lb lean pork shoulder, cut into 1-in cubes
2 tablespoons soy sauce
¼ teaspoon pepper
1 cup boiling water
8 oz mushrooms, quartered
2 tablespoons cornstarch
4 tablespoons water

394 calories per serving
Heat oil with salt and gently cook pork until golden brown, approximately 8 minutes. Add soy sauce, pepper and boiling water, cover and simmer for 5 minutes. Mix cornstarch with water and pour into pork mixture, stirring continuously for 5 minutes. Garnish with chopped parsley and serve with boiled rice. *Serves 4.*

Casserole of belly of pork

1 lb lean belly of pork
2 onions
1 carrot
1 stalk celery
salt, pepper
mixed herbs
1 cup chicken stock (or use bouillon cube)
1 tablespoon tomato purée or paste

Suitable for dieters: 166 calories per serving
Trim off fat from the belly of pork. Place in a casserole and add chopped onions, celery, carrot, seasoning, tomato purée, herbs and stock. Cook for 1½–2 hours in a moderate oven, 350°F, 180°C. Skim off any surplus fat and serve. *Serves 4.*

Deviled chicken

4 chicken portions
seasoned flour
2 tablespoons cooking oil
8 oz shallots or onions
mixed herbs
1 teaspoon curry powder
pinch cayenne
1 cup stock
2 oz mushrooms

338 calories per serving
Roll chicken pieces in seasoned flour and fry in oil till golden brown. Add shallots or sliced onions and fry. Add mixed herbs, curry powder, cayenne and stock. Simmer for 30–40 minutes, add mushrooms and cook for a further 15 minutes. *Serves 4.*

Chicken fricassée

2 cups Béchamel sauce:
2 cups skim milk
1 small carrot
1 small onion
1 small piece celery
1 blade mace, 4 cloves
6 white peppercorns
2 oz polyunsaturated margarine
4 tablespoons flour
salt
1 uncooked chicken or 4 chicken pieces

390 calories per serving
Peel and cut vegetables into pieces and put in a saucepan with milk, salt, mace, peppercorns and cloves. Infuse for at least ½ hour, then strain. Melt margarine in a saucepan, add flour and cook well without browning. Add seasoned milk gradually, stirring all the time, and boil for 3–5 minutes. Cut chicken into joints and remove skin. Put in casserole and add hot sauce. Simmer gently for 1–1½ hours. With cooked chicken pieces the cooking time need only be ½ hour. Mushrooms may be added. *Serves 4–6.*

Coq au vin

½ cup cooking oil
4 chicken pieces
8 oz onions, chopped
4 oz lean bacon, diced
1 clove garlic, crushed
1 cup stock
¼ teaspoon mixed herbs
2 bay leaves
4 peppercorns
salt
2 cups red Burgundy
4 oz mushrooms, halved
4 tablespoons flour

446 calories per serving
Heat 2 tablespoons oil and lightly brown chicken pieces, onions and bacon with garlic. Add stock, herbs, bay leaves, peppercorns, salt and Burgundy, cover and simmer until chicken is cooked, about 30 minutes. Add mushrooms and simmer for 20 minutes. Remove chicken to a serving dish; strain sauce, placing onions, bacon and mushrooms on top of chicken; keep warm, reserve liquid. Heat remaining oil, add flour, stirring well, and cook for 1 minute without browning. Gradually add reserved liquid, stirring all the time. Simmer for 1 minute, then pour on top of chicken. Serve with creamed potatoes and broccoli spears. *Serves 4.*

Romany chicken

4 tablespoons cooking oil
4 chicken pieces
12 oz onions, sliced
14-oz can tomatoes
1 teaspoon salt
¼ teaspoon pepper, bay leaf
2 tablespoons flour
½ cup liquid skim milk
1 teaspoon granulated sugar

Suitable for dieters, if flour omitted: 275 calories per serving.
Heat oil and fry chicken pieces gently until golden brown. Remove chicken from pan and sauté onions without browning for 10 minutes. Add tomatoes, salt, pepper and bay leaf. Place chicken joints in mixture, cover and simmer gently for about 30 minutes. Remove chicken pieces to a serving dish and keep warm. Mix flour with milk and add to pan. Stir continuously until mixture thickens. Add sugar and cook for 5 minutes. Remove bay leaf, pour over chicken and serve. *Serves 4.*

Chicken à la Sabra

1 cut-up frying chicken (about 2 lb)
salt and pepper
paprika
1 large onion, sliced
6 tablespoons cooking oil
1 cup orange juice
¼ cup white cooking wine (optional)
boiled rice
1 teaspoon curry powder
chopped mint or dill

510 calories per serving
Season chicken with spices. Brown onion and chicken in oil. Add orange juice and cook slowly, uncovered, for about 45 minutes, or until tender. Add wine and heat a few minutes. Taste and adjust seasoning. Serve on boiled rice, seasoned with curry powder. Top with mint or dill. For buffet service, remove bones from chicken when tender. Cut chicken into bite-size pieces. Reheat in sauce and add wine. *Serves 4.*

Pineapple chicken cakes

6 oz chicken, cooked and finely diced
1 small can pineapple rings
2 oz potatoes, boiled and mashed, or 5 tab-
    lespoons instant potato flakes
¼ cup onions, finely chopped
grated rind of ½ lemon
salt and pepper
egg white and breadcrumbs, for coating
¾ cup cooking oil

308 calories per serving
Marinate cooked diced chicken in pineapple juice for 1 hour. Mix chicken and pineapple juice with potato, onion, lemon rind, salt and pepper. Divide mixture into four parts and form into round cakes placing pineapple rings in center. Coat with egg white and breadcrumbs. Heat oil and fry cakes until evenly browned on both sides. Drain well on paper towels. *Serves 4.*

Breast of chicken sauté

2 large chicken breasts, cut in half
3 tablespoons cooking oil
¼ cup chopped onions
½ cup sliced mushrooms
½ cup dry white wine
salt and pepper
white seedless grapes for garnish

Suitable for dieters: 261 calories per serving
Season chicken breasts with salt and pepper and sauté until lightly browned in the oil. Add onions, mushrooms and white wine. Cover and cook on low heat for about 30–40 minutes, or until chicken is tender. Serve with sauce from pan and garnish with white seedless grapes.
Serves 4.

Chicken with Amandine sauce

1 frying chicken (2½–3 lb), cut into pieces
¼ cup slivered almonds
4 tablespoons cooking oil
½ teaspoon salt
2 tablespoons lemon juice
½ teaspoon minced scallions
salt, pepper, powdered ginger

356 calories per serving
Pre-heat oven to 350°F, 180°C. Season chicken with salt, pepper and a pinch of powdered ginger. Place chicken, skin-side down, in baking dish and bake for about 40–60 minutes. Turn once during baking and baste either with juice in dish or with some fat-free chicken stock. If necessary for browning, raise temperature to 450°F, 230°C, for the last 10 minutes of cooking. Just before chicken is done prepare sauce. Sauté almonds in oil until lightly browned. Add lemon juice, salt and onion. Pour over chicken or serve separately.   *Serves 4.*

Lemon chicken

1 frying chicken (2½–3 lb), cut into serving
   pieces
4 tablespoons cooking oil
6 tablespoons fresh lemon juice
rind of 1 lemon, grated
1 crushed clove garlic
½ teaspoon salt
dash of pepper
chopped parsley

Suitable for dieters: 236 calories per serving
Arrange chicken in shallow casserole or baking dish. Pour lemon, garlic, salt, pepper and oil mixture over chicken. Cover and bake at 350°F, 180°C, until tender, about 45–50 minutes. Uncover casserole the last 10 minutes to allow chicken to brown. Baste occasionally during cooking. Before serving, sprinkle with chopped parsley.   *Serves 4.*

Chicken bake (illustrated opposite)

1 chicken (3–3½ lb)
4 tablespoons seasoned flour
2–4 tablespoons cooking oil
1 clove garlic, crushed
1 medium onion, sliced
1 lb carrots, sliced
1 lb potatoes, sliced
1 lb leeks, sliced
2 cups chicken stock, or water and bouillon
  cube
bay leaf, bouquet garni
2 tablespoons cornstarch for thickening

Suitable for dieters: 302 calories per serving
Joint chicken. Remove fat. Roll in seasoned flour, brown quickly in oil. Place in stock, simmering gently. Soften vegetables in oil in covered pan with garlic. Add to casserole. Cook in oven at 274°F, 140°C, for 1½–2 hours. Skim off any fat, then thicken with cornstarch mixed with ¼ cup cold water. *Serves 6.*

A meal in itself. Serve dieters only allowed quantity of potatoes.

Chicken Jambalaya (illustrated opposite)

¾ cup cooking oil
4 chicken pieces
8 oz ham, diced
1 green pepper, chopped
8 oz onions, chopped
1 clove garlic, crushed
⅓ cup long-grain rice
2 cups stock
salt and pepper
1 small package frozen peas
chopped pimentoes for garnish

609 calories per serving
Heat the oil and lightly brown the chicken pieces and ham. Add the green pepper, onions and garlic and sauté without browning for 5 minutes. Add the rice, stock, salt and pepper, cover and simmer until cooked, approximately 20 minutes. Add the peas and simmer for 10 minutes. Serve with chopped pimentoes and tossed mixed salad as shown in dish at top right of picture. *Serves 4.*

Chicken apricot (illustrated opposite)

4 chicken pieces, trimmed of fat
1-lb can apricots or for dieters: 1 lb apricots,
  poached in water with artificial sweetener
2 tablespoons Worcestershire sauce
juice of 1 lemon
2 tablespoons cornstarch
seasoning

293 calories per serving
Season chicken and put in baking dish. Mix juice from apricots with Worcestershire sauce and lemon juice. Cover with tight lid. Bake at 350°F, 180°C, for 50 minutes. Mix cornstarch with 2 tablespoons cold water. Add to juice in baking dish. Arrange apricots around dish. Bake uncovered until gravy thickens and apricots are slightly browned, about 10–15 minutes.
Serves 4.

Eggplant with tomato sauce (illustrated opposite)

2 medium-sized eggplants
2 tablespoons cornstarch, seasoning
1 egg white, lightly beaten
2 tablespoons white breadcrumbs
oil for deep frying

Tomato sauce:
  2 tablespoons oil
  1 onion, finely chopped
  4 level tablespoons tomato purée
  15-oz can tomatoes
  1 level teaspoon sugar
  $\frac{1}{4}$ level teaspoon basil, seasoning
  $\frac{1}{2}$ cup red wine

Suitable for dieters: 94 calories per serving
To make sauce: heat oil, add onion and sauté until soft, without browning. Stir in tomato purée, tomatoes, seasoning, sugar, basil and red wine. Cover and simmer 20 minutes. Rub through sieve or blend. Reheat and serve separately. Peel eggplants and slice diagonally. Coat with cornstarch, to which salt and pepper have been added. Dip in beaten egg white, drain and coat with breadcrumbs. Heat oil to 375°F, 190°C. Add eggplant slices and fry until browned. Drain on paper towels. Sprinkle with salt and pile into warmed serving dish. Serve with tomato sauce. *Serves 4.*

Stuffed peppers (illustrated opposite)

4 peppers
8 oz ground raw beef
4 oz mushrooms, sliced, or small whole
  button mushrooms
2 shallots, chopped
4 tablespoons oil
2 tomatoes, peeled and sliced
2 level tablespoons cornstarch
$\frac{1}{2}$ cup stock or water
pinch of thyme
seasoning

202 calories per serving
Cut slice from stem end of each pepper. Carefully remove seeds and membrane from peppers. Blanch in boiling water for 5 minutes. Drain and cool. For filling: sauté beef, mushrooms and shallots in hot oil for a few minutes. Remove to bowl and add tomatoes. Pour off oil from pan, leaving about 2 tablespoons. Add cornstarch and mix well. Add stock, stir till boiling and boil for 1 minute. Pour over ingredients in bowl, add thyme and correct the seasoning. Fill peppers, replace lids and bake at 350°F, 180°C, for 15–20 minutes. *Serves 4.*

Spiced red cabbage (illustrated opposite)

6 tablespoons cooking oil
1 lb red cabbage, sliced
6 cloves, 1 bay leaf
1 small onion
4 tablespoons vinegar
2 tablespoons sugar
$\frac{1}{2}$ cinnamon stick, salt and pepper
1 cup stock
1 apple, peeled and diced

185 calories per serving
Heat oil and sauté cabbage without browning for 3 minutes. Stick cloves into onion and add to cabbage with bay leaf, vinegar, sugar, cinnamon stick, salt and pepper and simmer for 5 minutes. Add stock and apple, cover and simmer gently for 20 minutes. Remove the onion, bay leaf and cinnamon stick before serving. This dish is good with veal and pork casseroles. *Serves 4.*

Cauliflower casserole

1 head cauliflower
$\frac{2}{3}$ cup cooking oil
2 tablespoons chopped onion
$\frac{1}{3}$ cup cornstarch
3 cups skim milk
1 teaspoon salt
1$\frac{1}{2}$ teaspoons paprika
4 tablespoons chopped parsley
$\frac{1}{2}$ teaspoon Worcestershire sauce
1 clove garlic
$\frac{1}{2}$ cup breadcrumbs

385 calories per serving
Separate cauliflower into flowerets and arrange in casserole dish. Cook until tender, about 5 minutes, to keep the taste best and retain maximum vitamins. Heat 6 tablespoons oil in saucepan and sauté onion. Blend in cornstarch and stir in milk gradually until smooth and thick. Add parsley, salt, paprika and Worcestershire sauce and pour over the cooked cauliflower. Sprinkle breadcrumbs over top, either plain, or mixed with 2 tablespoons of oil heated with garlic, remove garlic. Good with roast dishes or ham.   *Serves 4.*

Stuffed summer squash

1 summer squash, medium size

Stuffing:
    8 oz ground raw beef or ground cooked beef or lamb
    4 tablespoons dried breadcrumbs
    1 chopped onion
    2 chopped tomatoes
    2 tablespoons tomato sauce
    salt, pepper, mixed herbs

Suitable for dieters: 167 calories per serving
Peel the squash and cut in two lengthwise. Remove seeds. Precook by boiling for 2 minutes or steaming for 5 minutes. Place on a fireproof dish. Mix all the stuffing ingredients together and fill the hollows in the squash. Cover with foil or greased paper and bake in a moderate oven, 350°F, 180°C, till tender.   *Serves 4.*

Ground ham, chopped corned beef or flaked canned fish can be used instead of ground beef or lamb. Mushrooms and /or celery may be added to the mixture.

Braised zucchini

1 lb zucchini
$\frac{3}{4}$ oz polyunsaturated margarine
salt and pepper, freshly ground
2 tablespoons hot water

Suitable for dieters: 50 calories per serving
Wash and slice the zucchini. Place in a casserole dish. Dot with margarine and season with salt and plenty of pepper. Add water. Cook in a moderate oven, 325°F, 160°C, for 45 minutes to 1 hour.   *Serves 4.*

Tomato and squash casserole

1 medium summer squash
8 tomatoes
2 large onions
seasoning and chopped parsley
½ clove garlic (optional), finely chopped or
  crushed

Suitable for dieters: 30 calories per serving
Peel squash, scoop out seeds and cut into slices.
Put alternate layers of sliced squash, tomato and
onion into a greased casserole. Season each layer.
Bake in a moderate oven, 375°F, 190°C, for 45
minutes or till tender.   *Serves 4.*

Vegetable mix

3 cups diced vegetables, e.g. green beans,
  carrots, rutabagas, turnips, cauliflower,
  onion, sprouts, cabbage
tomato juice
salt, pepper
chopped parsley or chives

Suitable for dieters: 50 calories per serving
Cook vegetables and drain. Season well and add
herbs. Bind with warmed tomato juice and
serve.   *Serves 2.*

Tomato sauce

1 onion
¼ cup carrot
½ oz lean bacon
½ oz polyunsaturated margarine
4–5 tomatoes, skinned or small can tomatoes or
  use tomato purée mixed with the stock
1 cup stock or liquid from canned tomatoes
salt, pepper
pinch sugar
1 tablespoon cornstarch if necessary

100 calories per serving
Slice onion and carrot and cut bacon into small
pieces. Melt margarine, add carrot, onion and
bacon and sauté lightly, then add the tomatoes.
Crush tomatoes down with a spoon and cook for
4–5 minutes. Add stock, season with salt and
pepper; cook for 40–45 minutes, stirring occasionally. Sieve or blend. Reheat and add sugar and
cornstarch dissolved in water if sauce is not thick
enough.   *Serves 3–4.*

Ratatouille

2 medium onions, sliced
6 tablespoons oil
1 eggplant, sliced
4 tomatoes, skinned and chopped
1 green and/or red pepper, prepared and diced
2 zucchini, sliced
salt and black pepper

135 calories per serving
This is basically a casserole of eggplants with other vegetables. The proportions can vary depending on availability and is even nice without the eggplants. Sauté the sliced onions in oil till soft, add the other prepared vegetables, season and simmer gently with lid on for ¾–1 hour.   *Serves 4–6.*

Sweet and sour beets

4 tablespoons cooking oil
4 tablespoons flour
2 tablespoons sugar
4 tablespoons vinegar
1 cup water
salt and pepper
1½ lb beets, cooked and diced

235 calories per serving
Heat oil, remove from heat and stir in flour. Add sugar and vinegar to water, blend into flour and oil, return to heat and bring to boil stirring all the time, then simmer for 3 minutes. Add salt, pepper and beets, cover and simmer gently for 5 minutes. This recipe goes well with lightly cooked lamb dishes.   *Serves 4.*

Spiced ham steaks

4 lean ham steaks
whole cloves
3 tablespoons mustard
½ cup brown sugar
2 tablespoons cider
½ cup cooking oil
1 small can pineapple rings

681 calories per serving
Remove rind and fat from ham steaks. Stick cloves into steaks. Mix mustard, brown sugar and cider together. Heat oil and sauté pineapple rings for approximately 4 minutes, turning once, remove from pan and keep warm. Cook ham for 5 minutes on one side, turn and coat cooked side with mustard mixture and cook for a further 5 minutes. Serve immediately with pineapple rings, watercress, sautéd potatoes and cauliflower.   *Serves 4.*

Ham and pineapple hot-pot

4 tablespoons cooking oil
1¼ lb lean cooked ham, diced
1¼ lb cooked potatoes, sliced
1-lb can pineapple cubes
salt, pepper
½ cup water
2 tablespoons flour
1 small package frozen peas, cooked
1½ teaspoons Worcestershire sauce
¼ teaspoon Tabasco sauce

314 calories per serving
Heat oil and gently sauté ham and potatoes for 3 minutes. Make pineapple juice up to 1 cup with water and add to ham and potatoes. Add salt and pepper, cover and simmer for 15 minutes. Mix flour to smooth paste with ½ cup of water and pour into ham mixture, stirring continuously; simmer for 3 minutes. Add pineapple cubes, peas, Worcestershire and Tabasco sauces, simmer for 5 minutes. Serve with creamed potatoes and carrots. *Serves 6.*

Ham risotto

6 tablespoons cooking oil
6 oz ham, diced, lean
8 oz onions, finely chopped
4 oz mushrooms, chopped
8 oz tomatoes, skinned and chopped
¾ cup long-grain rice
1 teaspoon tomato purée
1½ cups stock (fat removed)
salt, pepper

488 calories per serving
Heat oil and sauté ham and onions until tender but not brown. Add mushrooms, tomatoes and rice and cook gently for 5 minutes, stirring all the time. Mix tomato purée with stock, add salt and pepper and pour into mixture in pan. Bring to boil. Cover and simmer, stirring occasionally until rice is cooked and liquid absorbed, approximately 15 minutes. Serve with watercress salad. *Serves 4.*

Cold Main Dishes And Salads

For an easy summertime meal, there is little to compare with the flavor of home-cooked lean cold meats, a simple tossed salad and a potato in its jacket. Because salads play such a large part in the good-hearted diet, it is useful to know a wide selection, ranging from the straightforward to the exotic. Meat loaves and galantines are a good way of making economical dishes more interesting. Although they are a little time-consuming to make, it is well worth while because you can ensure they contain all the correct ingredients and subtle flavorings. They also make a pleasant change from bought continental cold meats, which are not allowed because they contain too much fat.

Deviled beef rolls

4 tablespoons oil
1 onion, chopped
2 tablespoons cornstarch
1 level teaspoon curry powder
1 beef bouillon cube
$\frac{1}{2}$ cup water
salt, pepper
2 tablespoons chutney
4 level tablespoons fresh breadcrumbs
4 slices cooked beef, $1\frac{1}{2}$ oz each at the most

215 calories per serving
Heat oil and sauté onion until soft. Add cornstarch curry powder and bouillon cube. Gradually stir in water, bring to boil and cook for 1 minute, stirring all the time. Season and add chutney and breadcrumbs. Leave to cool. Spread mixture on slices of beef and roll up. Serve cold with salad. *Serves 4.*

Salmon loaf

two 8-oz cans salmon
4 tablespoons skim milk
2 tablespoons grated onion
4 tablespoons lemon juice
$\frac{1}{2}$ teaspoon salt
pinch cayenne
4 tablespoons chopped green pepper
4 tablespoons chopped celery
$\frac{1}{2}$ cup arrowroot cookie crumbs
1 egg white

Suitable for dieters: 133 calories per serving
Drain salmon and measure liquid; make up to $\frac{1}{2}$ cup with skim milk. Add onion, lemon juice, salt, cayenne, green pepper, celery, arrowroot cookie crumbs and egg white. Mix well and spoon into a greased loaf pan and bake at 350°F, 180°C, for 1 hour. Allow to cool for 5 minutes before removing from the pan. *Serves 4.*

Salmon crunch

8-oz can red salmon
salt, pepper
pinch nutmeg
$\frac{2}{3}$ cup special mayonnaise (page 68)
1 small cucumber
4 tablespoons oil
2 slices white bread, diced
lettuce

247 calories per serving
Flake salmon and remove any skin or bone. Add seasonings and mayonnaise and blend together. Dice half the cucumber, fold into salmon mixture and chill. Heat oil and fry bread until golden brown. Drain on paper towels. Fold into the salmon mixture and serve immediately on a bed of lettuce garnished with twists of cucumber. *Serves 4.*

Yorkshire meat loaf

8 oz stew beef
4 oz lean bacon
$\frac{2}{3}$ cup white breadcrumbs
1 egg white
salt, pepper
pinch of sage and marjoram

194 calories per serving
Grind meat with bacon and mix with crumbs. Add seasonings and herbs and blend with egg white. Grease a metal bowl, put in the mixture and spread smoothly on top. Cover with waxed paper. Tie down and steam for $2\frac{1}{2}$–3 hours. Cool in the bowl for a little, then turn out and leave till quite cold. Serve with salad. Two tablespoons minced onion can be used instead of the herbs if preferred.   *Serves 6.*

Ham ring mold

6 teaspoons powdered gelatine
$\frac{1}{4}$ cup hot water
16-oz can tomato juice
2 teaspoons sugar
salt, pepper
1 cup diced celery
1 cup grated carrot
8 oz lean, diced ham

Suitable for dieters: 136 calories per serving
Dissolve gelatine in hot water, add to tomato juice, add sugar, salt and pepper to taste. Leave to thicken, then stir in carrot and celery. Place in a ring mold. Chill. Unmold on shredded lettuce, fill center with ham. Garnish with salad in season.   *Serves 3–4.*

Salmon mousse (illustrated opposite)

two 8-oz cans red salmon (or tuna fish)
$\frac{1}{4}$ cup fresh breadcrumbs
$\frac{1}{2}$ cup skim milk
2 heaped tablespoons chopped parsley
$\frac{1}{2}$ teaspoon salt
dash cayenne
2 tablespoons lemon juice
2 tablespoons Worcestershire sauce
1 tablespoon powdered gelatine
2 egg whites
capers for garnish

Suitable for dieters: 185 calories per serving
Drain salmon into large basin, reserving juice. Remove any skin and bone; flake flesh. Put milk and breadcrumbs into small saucepan and add salmon juice. Cook mixture over low heat, stirring, for about 5 minutes. Add to salmon with lemon juice, seasoning and minced parsley. Melt gelatine in a little warm water; add to mixture. Beat egg whites till very stiff and fold into mixture. Oil a basin or ring mold, fill with mixture and cover top with a round of waxed paper. Set in a pan with hot water quarter-way up the side of the bowl. Bake in pre-heated oven, 350°F, 180°C, for 40–45 minutes. A ring mold looks attractive as the center can be filled with capers or parsley sauce, or sauce can be served separately. Serves 4–6.

Quick aspic (illustrated opposite)

3 teaspoons powdered gelatine
$\frac{1}{4}$ cup hot water
1 cup low-fat stock, gravy or soup
3 cups lean, cooked meat, cut in small
   pieces
salt, pepper, nutmeg
2 hard-boiled egg whites

Suitable for dieters: 82 calories per serving
Dissolve gelatine in hot water, add to stock. Season meat with salt, pepper and nutmeg. Pack in bowl or loaf pan with slices of hard-boiled egg whites. Add gelatine mixture. Leave to set in refrigerator or cool place. Serve in slices with salads.   Serves 6.

Tomato meat loaf (illustrated opposite)

1 lb ground lean beef
$\frac{1}{2}$ cup breadcrumbs
8 oz grated carrot
1 teaspoon prepared mustard
2 tablespoons Worcestershire sauce
4 tablespoons tomato sauce
salt, pepper
1 egg white

Suitable for dieters: 148 calories per serving
Mix all ingredients together. Line a loaf or 7-in cake pan with greased waxed paper. Cook 1$\frac{1}{2}$ hours at 300°F, 150°C, standing in a pan of water in the oven. The water should be half-way up the outside of the pan. Leave till cold. Serve with tomato quarters and mixed salad.   Serves 8.

Summer rice salad (illustrated opposite)

1 cup cold cooked rice
2 cups chopped cooked chicken and/or ham
¼ cucumber, sliced
1 medium onion, chopped finely
1 green pepper, cut in strips
small can corn, drained
4 tablespoons French dressing
small carton low-fat natural yogurt
juice of lemon to taste
chopped chives to garnish
freshly ground pepper

Suitable for dieters: 182 calories per serving
Combine rice with meat and salad vegetables. Mix French dressing with yogurt and lemon juice to taste. Mix everything thoroughly. Spoon onto serving dish. Garnish with chives and freshly ground pepper. *Serves 8.*

A radish and curly endive salad, pictured top left, is a good accompaniment that turns this into a delicious main course for a summer supper party.

New Zealand fish salad (illustrated opposite)

4 fish steaks, preferably salmon
8 oz new potatoes
4-oz package frozen string beans
1 lettuce
8 oz shredded carrots
½ sliced cucumber
8 slices orange
¼ cup French dressing

With dressing: 441 calories per serving
Without dressing: 304 calories per serving
Cook potatoes and beans and leave to cool. Broil fish steaks and cool. Line serving dish with lettuce leaves. Fill with sliced cold potatoes, beans, carrots and cucumber. Place fish in center. Decorate with orange. Sprinkle with dressing and serve. *Serves 4.*

Piquant roast beef salad (illustrated opposite)

1 cup cold roast beef
6 tablespoons oil
2 tablespoons wine vinegar
1½ level teaspoons dry mustard
1 teaspoon anchovy paste
2 teaspoons chopped capers
2 level tablespoons chopped chives
2 level tablespoons chopped parsley
black pepper

Suitable for dieters: 225 calories per serving
Cut beef into small strips. Blend oil, vinegar, mustard and anchovy paste thoroughly. Add capers, chives, parsley and pepper. Marinate meat in this dressing for about 1 hour. Garnish with extra chopped parsley. Serve with green salad. *Serves 4.*

Low-cholesterol mayonnaise

2 tablespoons cornstarch
$\frac{3}{4}$ cup skim milk
$\frac{1}{2}$ teaspoon salt
2 teaspoons sugar
1 teaspoon dry mustard
$\frac{1}{2}$ teaspoon paprika
$\frac{1}{4}$ cup oil
$\frac{1}{4}$ cup vinegar or lemon juice

689 calories
Mix cornstarch to a paste with milk. Cook until thickened. Place in bowl with salt, sugar, mustard and paprika. Beat well until smooth. Add a tablespoon of oil and a tablespoon of vinegar, beating constantly. Continue adding alternate tablespoons of oil and vinegar until mixture is complete and well blended.

Summer mold

1 chicken bouillon cube
1 cup hot water
2 level tablespoons powdered gelatine
$\frac{1}{4}$ teaspoon Tabasco sauce
6 tablespoons lemon juice
$\frac{2}{3}$ cup special mayonnaise (page 68)
$\frac{1}{4}$ small onion, finely chopped
2–3 sticks celery, chopped
1 red peeled apple, chopped
$\frac{1}{4}$ cup cooked peas
1–1$\frac{1}{2}$ cups cooked chicken, diced
watercress, slices of red apple

With mayonnaise: 196 calories per serving
Without mayonnaise: 138 calories per serving
Add hot water to chicken bouillon cube and stir well. Dissolve gelatine in hot stock. Stir in Tabasco sauce and lemon juice. Leave to cool, but not set. Gradually stir in mayonnaise. When setting add onion, celery, apple, peas and chicken. Turn into wet 6$\frac{1}{2}$-in ring mold and leave to set. Turn out on serving dish. Garnish with slices of apple and watercress.   Serves 4–6.
    Suitable for dieters if mayonnaise is left out.

Salmon or chicken mold

1 cup prepared aspic
$\frac{1}{2}$ cucumber, thinly sliced
2 hard-boiled egg whites, sliced
8-oz can salmon or similar amount finely
    chopped cooked chicken
8 oz cottage cheese
4 tablespoons special mayonnaise (page 68)
salt and pepper
2 tablespoons chopped dill pickle

Suitable for dieters: 164 calories per serving
Pour $\frac{1}{4}$-in layer of aspic into 1$\frac{1}{2}$-pt oval dish. Chill. When set arrange slices of cucumber and egg white on base. Chill. Pour another $\frac{1}{4}$-in layer of aspic on top. Chill. Mix together remaining aspic, chopped egg white, flaked salmon, cottage cheese, mayonnaise, seasoning and chopped dill pickle. Turn into dish and chill. Turn out onto a plate and serve, surrounded with shredded lettuce.   Serves 4.

Chicken galantine

1 cup hot stock
salt and freshly ground pepper
parsley, thyme
½ bay leaf
1 teaspoon powdered gelatine
4 tablespoons cold water
slices of cucumber
¼ cup cooked peas
1½ cups cooked chicken, turkey or rabbit
¼ cup ground ham

Suitable for dieters: 142 calories per serving
Infuse herbs and bay leaf in seasoned stock for 10 minutes. Add gelatine to the cold water; stand for 5–10 minutes, then dissolve over hot water. Strain stock. Add dissolved gelatine. Arrange cucumber slices and peas in base of mold or serving dish. Add chicken, cut into small pieces, and ground ham. Pour over gelatine mixture when it begins to thicken. Set in refrigerator. Serve with tossed salad.   *Serves 6.*

This is an attractive-looking dish when made in a ring mold.

Meat and tomato aspic

1 tablespoon powdered gelatine
½ cup cold water
¾ cup tomato purée (small can of purée can
    be diluted with added water)
1 onion, sliced
2 cloves
pinch mixed herbs
salt, pepper
1½ cups cooked meat, ground or finely
    chopped

Suitable for dieters: 138 calories per serving
Add gelatine to cold water in small bowl. Leave to stand for 5–10 minutes. Stand bowl in pan of hot water until gelatine dissolves. In separate pan boil tomato purée, onion, cloves and herbs. Add dissolved gelatine and seasoning. Strain. Add meat. Place in shallow dish and set in refrigerator. Serve with tossed salad.   *Serves 6.*

Vegetable vinaigrette

2 cups mixed vegetables: celery, leeks,
    beans, carrots, cucumber, mushrooms, etc.
1 chicken bouillon cube
1½ cups boiling water

Vinaigrette dressing:
    4 tablespoons vinegar
    ½ level teaspoon salt, pepper
    ¼ level teaspoon dry mustard
    little finely chopped parsley
    8 tablespoons corn oil

Suitable for dieters: 153 calories per serving
Prepare vegetables, then dice, and poach until tender in the stock made by dissolving chicken bouillon cube in boiling water. Do not overcook vegetables as they should retain their shape. Strain and leave to cool, then pour the dressing over. To make dressing: mix vinegar with seasonings, add oil and parsley and whisk with fork.   Serves 4.

American salad

1 head of lettuce
8 oz cottage cheese

Dressing:
    4 tablespoons oil
    2 tablespoons vinegar
    ¼ level teaspoon salt
    1 level teaspoon sugar

A few of these for garnish: pineapple
    chunks, slices of peach, apple radishes,
    watercress, walnuts (chopped)

Suitable for dieters: 151 calories per serving
Put dressing ingredients in screw-top jar and shake well. Toss lettuce leaves in a little dressing and arrange on 4 individual plates. Place cottage cheese in center of each and garnish with fruit and vegetables. Sprinkle with chopped walnuts and serve remaining dressing separately.   Serves 4.

Apple and olive salad

2 eating apples
2 tablespoons lemon juice
10–12 stuffed olives
6 radishes, sliced
1 small green pepper
lettuce

French dressing:
    4 tablespoons oil
    2 tablespoons vinegar
    pinch sugar, salt, pepper

Suitable for dieters: 150 calories per serving
Mix ingredients for French dressing well together. Core and finely chop apples. Toss in lemon juice; add stuffed olives, radishes, seeded and finely chopped green pepper. Toss all ingredients in French dressing. Serve on a bed of lettuce.   Serves 3–4.

Zucchini salad

1 lettuce
4 small zucchini
1 small onion
2 tomatoes
1 green pepper
1 clove garlic (optional)
salt, pepper
¼ cup French dressing or wine vinegar

With French dressing: 149 calories per serving. Suitable for dieters with wine vinegar: 19 calories per serving
Wash lettuce and tear up into small pieces. Slice the zucchini, onion, green pepper and cut tomato into wedges. Rub the serving bowl with garlic. Toss all the vegetables in the French dressing. Season with salt and pepper and pile into serving bowl. *Serves 4.*

Carrot and horseradish salad

1 lb carrots
1 eating apple
2 level tablespoons prepared horseradish or fresh grated horseradish

Dressing:
4 level tablespoons corn oil
4 level tablespoons white wine vinegar
salt and pepper
½ level teaspoon sugar

sprigs of parsley for garnish

Suitable for dieters: 136 calories per serving
Peel and grate carrots. Peel, core and grate apple. Mix together carrot, apple and horseradish and put into salad bowl. To make dressing: mix together corn oil, vinegar, salt, pepper and sugar. Pour over the salad. Garnish with sprigs of parsley. *Serves 3–4.*

Chicken Mexicana salad

4 tomatoes
1 green pepper, seeded and chopped
¾ cup long-grain rice, cooked and drained
1 cup cooked chicken, sliced

French dressing:
4 tablespoons corn oil
2 tablespoons vinegar
pinch sugar, salt and pepper

349 calories per serving
Mix ingredients for dressing well together. Chop tomatoes, leaving half for garnish. Mix tomatoes and pepper together and toss in French dressing. Lay cooked rice round edge of dish, then tomatoes and peppers. Lay sliced chicken in the center and garnish with tomato half. *Serves 4.*

Cucumber salad

1 lb brussels sprouts
1 small cucumber
1 carton low-fat natural yogurt
2 tablespoons special mayonnaise (page 68)
2 tablespoons lemon juice
salt and pepper

Suitable for dieters: 63 calories per serving
Remove damaged leaves from sprouts. Wash, dry and shred remaining leaves finely. Arrange in serving dish. Peel cucumber and dice finely. Combine yogurt with mayonnaise, lemon juice and seasoning to taste. Add cucumber to dressing and pile in serving dish. Garnish with sprinkling of red pepper.   *Serves 4.*

Pasta salad

$\frac{3}{4}$ cup small pasta shapes
1 small package mixed frozen vegetables
$\frac{1}{2}$ cucumber
2 tomatoes, skinned and seeded
$\frac{1}{2}$ cup French dressing

234 calories per serving
Cook pasta as directed on package in boiling salted water until just tender. Add mixed vegetables to pan of lightly salted boiling water, simmer for 2 minutes and drain. Allow to cool. Dice cucumber. Mix together cooked pasta, mixed vegetables, cucumber and tomato. Toss in French dressing before serving.   *Serves 4.*

Salad Romano

$1\frac{1}{2}$ cups long-grain rice
8-oz can tuna fish
$\frac{1}{2}$ cup cooked peas
1 red pepper, chopped
2–3 dill pickles, sliced
6–8 anchovy fillets, drained well

Dressing:
*   6 tablespoons corn oil*
*   2 tablespoons wine vinegar*
*   1 clove garlic, crushed*
* $\frac{1}{4}$ level teaspoon salt*
*   1 level teaspoon sugar*

342 calories per serving
Put all salad dressing ingredients in screw-top jar and shake well. Chill. Cook rice in boiling salted water until tender. Drain rice and rinse with hot water. Place in colander over simmering water for 5 minutes to remove moisture. Cool rice. Combine rice, flaked tuna fish, cooked peas, pepper and dill pickles and decorate with anchovy fillets.   *Serves 6.*

Grapefruit salad

2 fresh grapefruit
4 oz cottage cheese
chives or scallions, chopped
$\frac{1}{4}$ cup mandarin orange sections
$\frac{1}{2}$ eating apple, chopped
1 stalk celery, diced
$\frac{1}{2}$ green pepper, chopped

Dressing:
  6 tablespoons corn oil
  2 tablespoons vinegar
  $\frac{1}{4}$ level teaspoon salt
  1 level teaspoon sugar

Suitable for dieters: 158 calories per serving
Put all salad dressing ingredients in screw-top jar and shake well. To assemble the salad: cut each grapefruit in half then carefully remove grapefruit segments, cutting away pith. Remove any pith and skin from center of each half. Combine cottage cheese and chopped chives and place some in each grapefruit half. Combine grapefruit segments, mandarins, chopped apple, celery and pepper and toss all together in the prepared chilled dressing. Arrange this mixture in grapefruit halves and serve with extra salad as desired. *Serves 4.*

Tomato and orange salad

3 large oranges
1 lb tomatoes
1 container low-fat natural yogurt
4 tablespoons French dressing
seasoning

Suitable for dieters: 109 calories per serving
Peel oranges, cut into segments removing skin from each. Blanch tomatoes and remove skin. Cut into wedges. Arrange orange and tomato alternately in serving dish. Mix yogurt, dressing and seasoning together and pour over salad. Chill before serving. *Serves 4.*

Cauliflower salad (illustrated opposite)

1 medium cauliflower head
3 stalks celery, sliced
½ cup radishes, sliced (optional)
1 crisp apple, peeled and sliced
2 spring onions, sliced
1 red pepper, seeded and sliced
3 tablespoons chopped fresh herbs
1 cup French dressing, seasoned with
    crushed garlic
celery leaves for garnish

Suitable for dieters: 179 calories per serving
Wash cauliflower and divide into flowerets. Mix cauliflower with celery, radishes, apple, spring onions, sliced pepper and herbs, and chill in refrigerator. Toss in dressing. Garnish with celery leaves.   Serves 6.

Use cauliflower and celery as basis for this salad and vary the other ingredients according to season.

Tomato and anchovy salad (illustrated opposite)

4 large tomatoes
1 medium onion
large can anchovy fillets
chopped fresh chives or spring onion tops
½ cup oil
4 tablespoons wine vinegar
clove of garlic, crushed (optional)
salt and freshly ground pepper

274 calories per serving
Peel and thinly slice tomatoes and onion, and arrange on plate. Decorate with the anchovies. Sprinkle with dressing made from the oil, vinegar, garlic and seasoning. Garnish with chives.   Serves 4.

Spinach and bacon salad (illustrated opposite)

1 lb fresh spinach
2 lettuce hearts
6 oz lean bacon
8 oz cottage cheese

Dressing:
    1 teaspoon dry mustard
    ½ cup cooking oil
    ¼ cup wine vinegar
    salt and freshly ground pepper

515 calories per serving
Remove spinach stems. Wash spinach and lettuce leaves and tear or chop finely. Mix together. Fry bacon. When crisp, cool on paper towels to absorb excess fat. Crumble bacon and add to spinach. Mix dressing and use half to toss salad. Mix remaining dressing with cheese and place on serving dish. Surround with spinach mixture. Serves 4.

String beans vinaigrette (illustrated opposite)

1 beef bouillon cube
1½ cups boiling water
½ lb string beans, shredded

Vinaigrette dressing:
  6 tablespoons corn oil
  2 tablespoons vinegar
  ¼ level teaspoon salt
  pepper
  pinch dry mustard
  little finely chopped parsley

Garnish (optional):
  few radish slices
  few mushroom slices

Suitable for dieters: 118 calories per serving
Dissolve bouillon cube in boiling water then simmer shredded beans in this stock until tender. Drain and leave to cool. For dressing: put oil, vinegar and seasonings in screw-top jar and shake well, then add chopped parsley. Chill and shake again before using. Slice mushrooms and sprinkle with a little dressing. Pour dressing over and mix well with beans just before serving. Garnish with mushrooms and sliced radishes. *Serves 4.*

Coleslaw and fruit salad (illustrated opposite)

8 oz white cabbage, finely chopped and
  washed
¼ cup carrots, grated
1 red-skinned sweet apple, sliced
1 orange, segmented
½ cup special mayonnaise (page 68)
a few walnuts for garnish (optional)

With mayonnaise: 86 calories per serving
Without mayonnaise: 37 calories per serving
Mix cabbage, carrot, apple and orange segments together. Toss with the mayonnaise. Serve garnished with walnuts and thin apple slices. *Serves 4.*
   Suitable for dieters if wine vinegar and lemon juice is used instead of mayonnaise.

Chicory and orange salad (illustrated opposite)

2 oranges
2 heads chicory
½ cup French dressing
few chopped hazelnuts (optional)

165 calories per serving
Peel and slice oranges into rings. Slice chicory thinly. Mix with dressing. Garnish with nuts. *Serves 4.*

Leeks vinaigrette

1 lb small leeks
¼ cup wine vinegar
½ cup corn oil
salt and pepper
2 tablespoons chopped parsley

168 calories per serving
Clean leeks and cook in boiling salted water for 10 minutes or until just tender without being mushy. Drain well and place on serving dish. Beat vinegar, corn oil and seasonings together with fork. Pour vinaigrette dressing over the hot leeks, sprinkle with parsley. Serve cold.   *Serves 4.*

Stuffed prunes and dates

1 cup prunes or dates
few chopped nuts
few pieces preserved ginger, chopped
4 oz cottage cheese
1 head chicory

Suitable for dieters: 97 calories per serving
Remove stones from prunes or dates. Mix nuts and ginger with cottage cheese. Fill stoned prunes or dates with cheese mixture. Place on bed of very finely sliced chicory. Serve as side salad.
Serves 3.

Fruit and cheese medley

1–2 fresh peaches
small carton raspberries
4–6 Cos lettuce leaves
8 oz cottage cheese
sprig of watercress

Suitable for dieters: 71 calories per serving
Wash peaches and cut in wedges, removing stones. Wash lettuce and raspberries, if necessary. Arrange fruit and lettuce in sections around the cottage cheese. Garnish with watercress.
Serves 4.

Desserts, Hot And Cold

A delicate dessert makes a perfect finish to any meal. One of the best things about the good-hearted diet is that, unless you are also on a weight-losing campaign, you can still eat sweet things. Substituting artificial sweeteners for sugar means that dieters can also enjoy som of the lighter recipes. The most successful desserts are those that don't try to be a pale copy of a rich egg-yolk-and-cream concoction; they make exciting use of the things you *can* eat, with the added bonus of not sitting heavily on the stomach afterwards.

Unsweetened fruit salad (illustrated on page 65)

juice of 2 sweet oranges or ½ cup
  unsweetened orange juice
½ cup cold boiled water
3–4 oranges
2–3 apples
½ cup black grapes
½ cup green grapes
1 peach
sprigs of mint (in season)

Suitable for dieters: 56 calories per serving
Place juice and water in glass dish. Peel and slice oranges. Slice apples. Seed grapes. Peel and slice peach and add all ingredients to juice. Garnish with mint sprigs. Serve very cold.   *Serves 8.*

Lemon snow (illustrated on page 64)

rind and juice of 1½ lemons
3 tablespoons sugar
1 cup water
1 tablespoon powdered gelatine
1 egg white

With sugar: 53 calories per serving.   Suitable for dieters with sweetener: 13 calories per serving
Peel off the yellow part of the lemon rind, avoiding the white pith. Put rind in a small pan with sugar and water. Bring to boil and strain into the gelatine. Stir until gelatine has dissolved. Allow to cool, then chill until just beginning to set. Add lemon juice and egg white. Whisk until frothy. Pile into a glass dish or individual glasses. *Serves 4.*

Apricot amber

1 lb apricots, without stones
2 egg whites
6 tablespoons sugar or 6–7 tablets artificial
  sweetener

With sugar: 123 calories per serving.   Suitable
for dieters with sweetener: 34 calories per serving
Cook apricots, then purée. Add two-thirds sugar
or sweetener. Place in a fireproof dish. Beat egg
whites stiffly. Add rest of sugar or sweetener.
Beat into meringue. Place on top of apricot mixture and bake in cool oven, 250°F, 120°C, for 30
minutes until meringue is lightly brown. *Serves 4.*

Variation: *Apple amber*. Use 1 lb peeled apples,
cooked with a little lemon rind. Purée and continue as for Apricot amber.

Surprise meringue

1 lb peeled and cored cooking apples
½ cup stoned or seedless raisins
4–8 tablespoons superfine granulated sugar
juice of 1 or 2 oranges
2 tablespoons rum (or extra orange juice)
2 egg whites
4 tablespoons sugar

269 calories per serving
Slice apples and put into 2-pt shallow oven dish
with raisins, granulated sugar, orange juice and
rum, if chosen. Cover with lid of foil, cook in
cool oven, 300°F, 150°C, for 40 minutes or until
apples are tender, and remove from oven. Separately beat together whites until stiff and gradually whisk in half sugar. Then fold in remaining
sugar. Pile or pipe meringue over apples and
return to oven for about 35 minutes until meringue is set and light golden. Serve hot or cold.
Serves 4.

Alison's pavlova

3 egg whites
⅓ cup cold water
1 cup sugar
1 teaspoon vinegar
1 teaspoon vanilla extract
pinch salt
6 tablespoons cornstarch
fresh or canned peaches, strawberries or
raspberries

Pavlova: 297 calories per serving.   Filling: 63
calories per serving
Pre-heat oven to 400°F, 200°C. Beat egg whites
and cold water together for 3 or 4 minutes. Add
sugar, vinegar, vanilla extract and salt, and beat
until stiff. Sprinkle on cornstarch and beat for 2–3
minutes, no more. Spread in a circle, piled high in
the center, on prepared waxed paper on a cold
greased baking tray. Place in oven, turned down
to 250°F, 120°C. Leave oven door open until
heat reaches 250°F. Cook for 1½ hours. Cool.
Just before serving, decorate with sliced fruit.
Serves 4–6.

Lemon sherbert

1½ teaspoons unflavored gelatine
1½ cups skim milk
¾ cup sugar
½ cup lemon juice
1 teaspoon grated lemon rind
1 egg white, stiffly beaten

221 calories per serving
Soak gelatine in 2 tablespoons water for 5 minutes. Heat milk and sugar, add gelatine and stir until dissolved. Chill. Gradually stir in lemon juice and lemon rind. Pour into freezing tray, freeze to mush. Turn into chilled bowl and beat until fluffy, but not melted. Fold in stiffly beaten egg white. Return to freezer and freeze until firm. *Serves 4.*

Dieters' orange whip

½ cup hot water
2 tablespoons powdered gelatine
1½ natural orange juice
1 teaspoon lemon juice
sweetener

Suitable for dieters: 41 calories per serving
Dissolve gelatine in hot water but do not boil. Add sweetener and lemon juice to orange juice. Add dissolved gelatine and allow to thicken slightly. Beat with a rotary whisk or in electric blender. Place in a serving dish and put in refrigerator. *Serves 4.*

Orange cooler

2 tablespoons vanilla pudding mix
2 cups skim milk
pinch salt
1 level teaspoon grated orange rind
2 oranges
8 level tablespoons raspberry jelly
4 tablespoons water

252 calories per serving
Make sauce with first five ingredients. Pour into serving dishes and sprinkle tops with sugar to prevent a skin from forming. Leave to cool. Peel oranges, remove pith and seeds and divide into segments. Arrange oranges on top of custard. Melt jelly and water together over a low heat and pour it over the oranges. Leave to cool. *Serves 4.*

Apple mousse

1 lb cooking apples
cup water
4 tablespoons redcurrant jelly
1 egg white
ground cinnamon or nutmeg

80 calories per serving
Cook apples in water. Add redcurrant jelly to hot fruit, then purée in electric blender. Whisk egg white stiffly, then add to apple when cool. Divide mixture into four glasses. Sprinkle with cinnamon or nutmeg. Chill.   *Serves 4.*

Fruit meringue

1 cup thick fruit purée
sugar to taste
2 egg whites

123 calories per serving
Sweeten purée to taste. Beat egg whites until stiff. Fold half of this into purée and put in baking dish. Add 2 tablespoons sugar to remaining egg white and pile on top of fruit. Bake in slow oven until the meringue is set. Serve cold.   *Serves 4.*

Fruit whip

¼ cup skim milk powder
juice of 1 lemon
1 cup thick fruit purée
½ cup cold water
sugar to taste
cinnamon, nutmeg, ginger, almond extract,
  or grated orange rind

136 calories per serving
Combine milk powder and cold water and beat until smooth. Chill or refrigerate for 1 hour. Add lemon juice and beat like whipped cream. Fold in purée, sweetened to taste, and add flavorings, e.g. cinnamon, nutmeg, or ginger with apple, almond extract with apricot, or cinnamon or grated orange rind with plums or prunes. Divide into four glasses, or serve in glass bowl.   *Serves 4.*

Flummery

3 teaspoons flour
1 cup cold water
½ cup sugar
¼ cup lemon juice
3 teaspoons powdered gelatine
⅓ cup hot water

79 calories per serving
Mix flour to smooth paste with a little of the cold water. Add remainder to sugar, heat to boiling, add flour gradually, and lemon rind. Cook for five minutes, stirring constantly. Add lemon juice and gelatine dissolved in hot water. Leave until thickening slightly; beat to stiff cream. Place in serving bowl. Cool.   *Serves 4.*

Apple icebergs

8 oz cooking apples
1 cup water
⅓ cup sugar
3 tablespoons farina
1 cup cold custard, made with skim milk

234 calories per serving
Peel, core and slice apples. Cook them in water with sugar. When tender, rub all through sieve. Return to pan, sprinkle in farina while stirring, and boil, stirring, for 3 minutes. Turn into large bowl and beat for 1–2 minutes. Leave to cool. When nearly cold, beat again until white. Pour custard into glass bowl and arrange the apple mixture in rocky heaps on top. Serve as cold as possible.   *Serves 4.*

Baked fruit whip

3 cups cooked prunes
½ cup sugar
¼ cup orange juice
1 teaspoon grated orange peel
½ teaspoon cinnamon
4 egg whites

145 calories per serving
Remove stones from prunes and mash fruit to pulp. Add 4 tablespoons sugar, orange juice, orange peel and cinnamon, blend well. Add remaining sugar to egg whites; beat until stiff. Fold prune mixture into beaten egg whites. Pile lightly into a greased 3-pt casserole dish. Bake in moderate oven, 350°F, 180°C, for 20–30 minutes.   *Serves 6.*

Lemon water ice

2 large lemons
2 cups water
⅓ cup sugar or 6–7 tablets artificial
    sweetener
1 egg white

With sugar 70 calories per serving.   Suitable for dieters with sweetener: 12 calories per serving Wash lemons and grate rinds. Squeeze juice from lemons. Put rind, sugar and water in pan, bring to boil and simmer for 10 minutes. Cool. Add lemon juice. If using sweetener, add it now. Place in freezer and freeze until mushy. Stiffly whip egg white. Mix thoroughly into semi-frozen lemon mixture. Continue to freeze until stiff. Whip at intervals with a fork during freezing so egg white is well mixed and the water ice freezes smoothly, otherwise the mixture is inclined to separate. *Serves 4.*

Blackberry, raspberry or strawberry sherbert

¾ cup sugar or 6–7 tablets artificial
    sweetener
2 cups water
1 breakfast cup blackberry, raspberry or
    strawberry purée
dash of Angostura bitters (optional)
1 egg white

With sugar: 111 calories per serving.   Suitable for dieters with sweetener: 29 calories per serving Make syrup by boiling together sugar and water for 5 minutes. Sieve fruit carefully to remove seeds. Add Angostura to fruit mixture. Mix with syrup. For dieters' version, add sweetener to boiled water. Mix with the fruit purée. Freeze both versions and when mushy add stiffly beaten egg white. Continue to freeze, whipping at intervals to keep mixture smooth and prevent separation.   *Serves 4–6.*

Ice cream (1)

1 cup water
¾ cup skim milk powder
1 tablespoon vanilla pudding mix

123 calories per serving
Blend vanilla pudding mix with half milk powder and half water. Bring slowly to boil. Allow to cool. While custard is cooling, whisk together rest of water and milk powder, adding sugar to taste. Beat two mixtures together. Freeze to mushy consistency. Beat again until mixture doubles its volume. Freeze. Yields 1 pint. *Serves 4.*

Ice cream (2)

1 level teaspoon powdered gelatine
⅔ cup hot water
¾ cup skim milk powder
1 cup cold water
4–6 tablespoons sugar, according to taste
vanilla

166 calories per serving
Dissolve gelatine in hot water. Add cold water to milk powder and sugar. Beat. Add gelatine. Beat well to mix. Freeze to mush. Beat again until mixture doubles its volume. Flavor with vanilla to taste. Freeze. Yields 1 pint. *Serves 4.*

Ice cream variations

basic ice cream (2)
8-oz can strawberries or 4 tablespoons crystallized ginger
4 tablespoons crystallized ginger syrup or 2 heaped teaspoons instant coffee
2 tablespoons hot water

For strawberry variation, drain strawberries and purée before adding to basic mixture. For ginger variation, mix ginger ingredients with basic mixture. For coffee, dissolve instant coffee in water before adding to ice cream. If flavoring with a quantity of liquid, remember to omit the equivalent volume of cold water to keep ice cream at correct consistency.

Pie dough made with polyunsaturated margarine

3 oz polyunsaturated margarine
4 tablespoons cold water
$\frac{3}{4}$ cup flour
$\frac{1}{4}$ teaspoon salt

1259 calories
Cream margarine and water together using a fork. Sift flour and salt together and add to margarine. Mix thoroughly and form into a firm dough. Turn onto lightly floured surface and knead gently until smooth. Roll out to $\frac{1}{4}$-in thickness and use as required. *See note in recipe below.*

Pie dough made with oil

$\frac{1}{3}$ cup oil
2 tablespoons cold water
$\frac{1}{4}$ cup flour
$\frac{1}{4}$ teaspoon salt

1373 calories
Place the oil and water in a bowl. Sift together the flour and salt and gradually mix into the liquid with a fork until a manageable dough is formed. Turn on to a lightly floured board and knead gently until smooth. Roll out to $\frac{1}{4}$-in thickness and use as required.

NOTE: Both these pastry recipes give amounts that will line one 8-in flan ring, or make twelve $2\frac{1}{2}$-in tartlets, or cover one 8-in pie plate, or cover one $1\frac{1}{2}$-pt pie pan.

Crumble topping
for apple, apricot, rhubarb, etc.

1 cup flour
2 tablespoons farina
$\frac{1}{2}$ cup sugar
4 oz polyunsaturated margarine

556 calories per serving
Mix all ingredients together. Spread mixture over fruit. Bake until brown at 400°F, 200°C. *Serves 4.*

Apple and lemon soufflé

1 cup apple purée
grated rind of 1 lemon
2 egg whites
pinch salt
4 tablespoons sugar or use artificial
  sweetener

With sugar: 86 calories per serving.   Suitable for dieters with sweetener: 31 calories per serving
Add lemon rind to apple purée. Whip egg whites stiffly (when they are at room temperature). Add sugar or sweetener, a tablespoon at a time, beating continuously. Using a metal spoon, fold egg white into the apple, mixing thoroughly. Pour into a straight-sided soufflé dish. Bake in pre-heated oven, 425°F, 220°C, for 20-25 minutes, until soufflé rises and browns slightly on top. Serve immediately.   *Serves 4.*

Apple shortcake

1 cup flour
1 teaspoon baking powder
pinch salt
2 tablespoons sugar
½ cup cooking oil
4 tablespoons cold water
2 large cooking apples
brown sugar
cinnamon

549 calories per serving
Sieve flour, baking powder and salt into a bowl and add sugar. Beat oil and water together until creamy, and add to dry ingredients. Mix well, adding sufficient cold water to make a fairly stiff dough. Roll out half pastry thinly and line pie plate or 8-in cake pan. Cover with good layer of sliced apples, sprinkle with brown sugar and cinnamon, and top with layer of pastry. Seal edges, make slits in center, and bake in fairly hot oven, about 425°F, 220°C, for 30–40 minutes, or until pastry is an even, golden brown. Sprinkle with confectioner's sugar before serving. Serve hot or cold.   *Serves 4–6.*

Tangy blackberry flan

Biscuit base:
  ½ cup graham crackers, crushed
  2 tablespoons sugar
  2 oz polyunsaturated margarine

Filling:
  8-oz can blackberry
  ½ cup blackberry jello
  ½ cup natural yogurt

235 calories per serving
Melt margarine, stir in graham crackers and sugar. Press into an 8-in pie pan to cover sides and base. Drain blackberries and reserve juice. Use ⅓ cup juice and heat to boiling point. Add jello and stir until dissolved. Allow to cool slightly. Meanwhile arrange blackberries in flan case, reserving a few for decoration. Beat yogurt into cooled jello and pour into flan case. Leave in a cool place to set for about 1½ hours. Decorate with reserved blackberries.   *Serves 6.*

Orange yogurt flan

$\frac{1}{3}$ *cup oil*
4 tablespoons cold water
$\frac{3}{4}$ *cup flour*
$\frac{1}{4}$ *level teaspoon salt*
1 cup sugar
2 tablespoons cornstarch
juice and grated rind of 1 orange
2 cartons low-fat natural yogurt
2 egg whites
6 tablespoons sugar

589 calories per serving
Mix together oil and water with fork. Sieve together flour and salt. Gradually add to the oil and water mixture to form a rollable dough. Roll out between two sheets of waxed paper and use to line 8-in pie plate. Line with waxed paper and bake blind in hot oven, 400°F, 200°C, for 15–20 minutes. Blend together sugar, cornstarch, orange juice and rind. Place in a double boiler and stir in the yogurt. Cook over boiling water, stirring constantly, until thick and smooth. Pour into the flan case. Whip egg whites until stiff and dry. Add half sugar and beat slowly until blended. Fold in remaining sugar. Pile meringue on top of flan and bake in moderately hot oven, 375°F, 190°C, for 5–10 minutes until lightly brown. *Serves 4–6.*

Chiffon pie

1 can fruit (e.g. raspberries, pineapple
  chunks)
fruit juice +1 tablespoon lemon juice +water
  to 1 cup
4 tablespoons sugar
2 tablespoons powdered gelatine
2 egg whites
cold baked pie shell (7-in diameter)

383 calories per serving
Beat gelatine in a little cold fruit juice and dissolve in remainder of warmed juice and sugar. Add fruit and when nearly set fold in stiffly beaten egg whites. Pour into cold baked pie shell.   *Serves 4.*

Coffee milk jello

2 tablespoons powdered gelatine (or enough
  for 1 pt)
2 tablespoons hot water
$2\frac{1}{4}$ *cups skim milk*
2 tablespoons coffee flavoring or strong
  black coffee
sweetener

Suitable for dieters: 53 calories per serving
Dissolve gelatine in hot water but do not boil. Cool and stir into milk. Flavor with coffee and sweetener to taste.   *Serves 4.*
   $\frac{1}{2}$ teaspoon vanilla may be substituted for coffee.

Chiffon tart

Shell:
  4 oz polyunsaturated margarine
  4 tablespoons soft brown sugar
  ⅓ cup cornflakes, crushed

Filling:
  1 lb prunes, cooked
  ½ cup prune juice
  ⅓ cup sugar
  ¼ teaspoon salt
  1 tablespoon lemon juice
  rind of 1 lemon
  2 tablespoons gelatine
  3 tablespoons hot water
  2 beaten egg whites

609 calories per serving
Melt margarine and sugar together in medium-sized saucepan. Add crushed cornflakes and stir in with wooden spoon. Press mixture round base and sides of an 8-in pie plate. Chill well. Stone and chop prunes. Replace in saucepan and add prune juice, sugar, salt, lemon juice and rind and bring to boil. Place in blender and purée, or press through sieve with wooden spoon. Dissolve gelatine in hot water, add to prune mixture. When mixture is at setting point, fold in stiffly beaten egg whites. Pour into cornflake shell and allow to set.   *Serves 4.*

Baked apple

1 apple, 6 oz
sweetener to taste
mixed spice, cinnamon or nutmeg (optional)
4 tablespoons water

Suitable for dieters: 60 calories
Slice top off the apple and remove core. Sprinkle with spice and add sweetener. Replace top. Place in a heat-proof dish with 2 tablespoons water and cover with foil or lid. Bake for 30–45 minutes till soft at 350°F, 180°C.

Variation: stuff center of apple with spices and orange segments. Pour over sweetener mixed with water. Bake.   (70 calories.)

Fruit juice jello

½ package fruit-flavored jello
1 container low-fat natural yogurt
few pieces fresh fruit

100 calories per serving
Make jello in usual way. Chill it and before it sets, fold in 1 carton low-fat yogurt to 1 cup jello. Whip twice before it sets. Serve garnished with fresh fruit and more yogurt. Add soft fruit like strawberries, whole; slice oranges, apples and pears; seed grapes, or cut pineapple and melon into cubes.   *Serves 4.*

Low-cholesterol pancakes or fritter batter

½ cup flour
¼ teaspoon salt
1 egg white
1 cup skim milk
2 tablespoons sugar
lemon juice
cooking oil for frying

303 calories per serving
Sift flour and salt into bowl. Make well in center and drop in egg white. Add half milk and beat until smooth. Gradually add remaining milk, beating all the time until thin batter is obtained. Cook on hot oiled griddle or in pan in usual manner. Sprinkle with sugar and lemon juice. *Serves 4.*

Alternatively serve with maple syrup or with the following sauce.

Orange pancake sauce

juice and grated rind of 1 small orange
juice of 1 small lemon
4 tablespoons arrowroot
2 tablespoons honey or maple syrup
1 orange, chopped segments and grated rind

76 calories per serving
Make orange and lemon juice up to 1 cup with water. Mix arrowroot to smooth paste with a little fruit juice and water. Heat remaining juice, add syrup, stir until dissolved, then pour over arrowroot. Return to pan and cook, stirring well until sauce thickens. Add chopped orange segments and grated rind. Roll up pancakes and pour sauce over.   *Serves 4.*

Apple fritters

1 lb cooking apples
4 tablespoons flour
pinch salt
2 level tablespoons sugar
2 tablespoons oil
½ cup tepid water
1 egg white
a little cooking oil for frying

272 calories per serving

Peel, core and slice apples. Sift flour, salt and sugar into bowl. Make well in center and add oil and water. Stir to form smooth batter. Fold in stiffly beaten egg white. Heat oil to 375°F, 190°C. Coat apple rings in batter and sauté in heated oil for approximately 3–4 minutes. Drain well on paper towels. Sprinkle with sugar before serving. *Serves 4.*

Baked bananas with lemon sauce

½ oz polyunsaturated margarine
4 tablespoons soft brown sugar
pinch ground nutmeg or cinnamon
grated rind and juice of 1 lemon
4 level teaspoons cornstarch
6 tablespoons water
4 small bananas

109 calories per serving

Place margarine, sugar, nutmeg, lemon juice and rind into saucepan. Blend cornstarch with water and stir into pan. Bring to boil, stirring all the time. Peel bananas and add to pan, whole or cut into pieces as desired. Cover pan and cook gently for 10 minutes. Serve hot or cold. *Serves 4.*

Baked apricot soufflé

¾ oz polyunsaturated margarine
1½ tablespoons flour
1 cup fresh stewed apricots to provide ¼ cup
    purée and ½ cup juice or use canned
    apricots
2 tablespoons sugar
3 egg whites

Sauce:
    ½ cup apricot juice
    2 level teaspoons arrowroot
    sugar and coloring

165 calories per serving

Mix margarine, flour, apricot purée and juice and cook till thick. Cool. Add sugar and fold in stiffly beaten egg whites. Pour mixture into prepared soufflé dish and bake in a moderate oven, 350°F, 180°C, until well risen and firm, about 45 minutes to 1 hour. To make sauce: thicken apricot juice with arrowroot; add sugar and coloring. Serve in a sauce boat. *Serves 3–4.*

Rhubarb and ginger pie (illustrated opposite)

1½ lb rhubarb
2 tablespoons crystallized ginger, chopped
1 tablespoon sugar
6 oz pie dough
a little skim milk or beaten egg white for
  glazing

272 calories per serving

Prepare rhubarb and cut into 1-in lengths. Layer fruit, ginger and sugar in an 8-in pie pan. Roll out dough to measure at least 1 in larger than the pie pan. Lay ½-in strips around wetted rim of pan. Brush with water. Lay large piece of dough on top of fruit. Press edges gently together. Trim off surplus and flute the edges. Make a hole in the center for steam to escape. Brush with milk or beaten egg white. Bake at 375°F, 190°C, for 40–50 minutes, until golden brown. *Serves 4.*

Summer pudding (illustrated opposite)

8 oz fresh or frozen fruit
2–4 tablespoons sugar
½ cup water
stale bread or cake (4–6 slices of a large
  loaf)

167 calories per serving

The best fruits to use are raspberries, logan-berries, blueberries, red plums. Stew fruit with sugar and water until tender. Cut bread or cake into ¼-in thick slices. Cut strips or triangles to line a 1-pt bowl, reserving enough whole slices for lid. Half fill lined bowl with fruit, add a layer of bread or cake, then rest of fruit, and finally a lid of bread or cake. Pour over juice; cover with weighted plate to fit inside bowl. Chill for several hours. Unmold and garnish with fruit. Serve with skim milk custard. *Serves 4.*

Apple flan (illustrated opposite)

6 oz pie dough (page 86)
6 tablespoons apricot jam
1½ lb cooking apples
grated rind of ½ lemon
1 oz polyunsaturated margarine
1 tablespoon sugar
1–2 red-skinned eating apples
1 teaspoon water

409 calories per serving

Line 8-in flan ring with dough. Spread 1 table-spoon of jam over base. Peel, core and slice cook-ing apples and cook gently until soft. Purée apples, then stir in lemon rind, margarine and sugar. Spoon into flan case. Arrange sliced eating apple on top. Bake in a fairly hot oven, 375°F, 190°C, for 20 minutes, then reduce heat to 325°F, 160°C, for further 20 minutes. Sieve remaining jam, add water and bring to boil stirring con-tinuously. Spoon over top of flan.

NOTE: If the purée seems too wet thicken with a little cornstarch. *Serves 4.*

Snacks And Luncheon Dishes

This selection of easy recipes fills a problematical gap. Dishes using cheese and whole eggs are favorite stand-bys for snack meals, and when these two ingredients need to be restricted, finding something quick to take their place can be difficult. The recipes in this section can be used for light lunches or suppers and bolstered into main meal dishes with the accompaniment of vegetables or a salad. Some, like the savory flans, can also be used as starters for a party meal.

Smoked haddock flan (illustrated opposite)

6 oz pie dough (page 86)
8 oz smoked haddock, poached in a little
   milk until tender
1 small can corn, drained
2 tablespoons flour
1 oz polyunsaturated margarine
1 cup skim milk
salt and pepper

435 calories per serving
Use dough to line a 8-in flan ring. Bake blind at 375°F, 190°C, for 30 minutes. Drain haddock, flake with fork and mix with corn. Melt margarine in saucepan, stir in flour and cook for 1 minute. Gradually blend in skim milk to make thick white sauce. Remove pan from the heat. Combine sauce with haddock, season to taste and pour mixture into flan case. Garnish with tomato slices or lemon twists and serve.   Serves 4.

Ratatouille flan (illustrated opposite)

6 oz pie dough (page 86)
4 small zucchini, sliced
1 small eggplant, chopped or sliced
1 small green pepper, seeded and chopped
2 small onions, skinned and sliced
1 clove garlic (optional)
1 small can tomato purée
4 tablespoons oil
salt and pepper

284 calories per serving
Use dough to line a 8-in flan ring. Bake blind at 375°F, 190°C, for 25–30 minutes until golden brown. Meanwhile, place remaining ingredients in a large, strong saucepan, cover with lid and simmer gently for about 1 hour or until vegetables are soft. Pile the vegetable mixture into the flan case and serve hot or cold.   Serves 4.

Bacon flan (illustrated on page 94)

6 oz pie dough (page 86)
*2 rashers lean bacon, with rind and fat
    removed*
½ oz polyunsaturated margarine
1 small onion, chopped
1 small can mushrooms, drained
1 chicken bouillon cube
¾ cup hot water
5 tablespoons skim milk powder
2 egg whites
¼ teaspoon oregano
salt and pepper
1 tomato, sliced

450 calories per serving
Use dough to line a 8-in flan ring. Bake blind at 375°F, 190°C, for 10 minutes. Broil bacon and chop into small pieces. Heat margarine and gently sauté onion until tender. Mix together the bacon, onion and mushrooms and place in flan case. Dissolve bouillon cube in hot water. Beat in dried milk and egg whites until thoroughly blended. Add oregano and season with salt and pepper. Pour this mixture into flan case and top with slices of tomato. Bake the flan at 375°F, 190°C, for 20–25 minutes or until golden brown and set. Serve hot or cold. *Serves 4.*

Cheese, oatmeal and tomato pie

*pie dough to line 7-in diameter, 1-in deep
    flan dish (page 86)*
1 oz polyunsaturated margarine
2 tablespoons oatmeal
*1 cup bottled tomato pulp or 6 canned
    peeled tomatoes*
2 tablespoons tomato juice
salt, pepper, mustard, parsley
*6 portions Romano or Parmesan cheese,
    grated*

1219 calories per serving
Line flan dish thinly with dough. Melt margarine in saucepan, blend in oatmeal, stirring well with wooden spoon. Gradually add tomato until mixture is soft and creamy. Cook well, stirring all the time, add seasonings and grated cheese. Put mixture in pie shall, bake in moderately hot oven, 375°F, 190°C, for 20–30 minutes until golden brown. Serve at once, garnished with parsley. *Serves 3.*

Cornish pasties

1 cup flour
4 oz polyunsaturated margarine
1 teaspoon baking powder
cold water

Filling:
½ cup finely chopped meat
½ cup raw potato, grated
¼ cup onion, finely chopped
*salt, pepper, pinch off a beef bouillon
    cube*

505 calories per serving
Rub fat into flour and baking powder. Mix with cold water to stiff dough. Roll out dough and cut 4 circles 6 inches in diameter. Mix filling ingredients and divide between pastry circles. Moisten edges with water and fold over in half. Crimp edges securely together. Bake for 15 minutes at 400°F, 200°C, then reduce heat to 325°F, 160°C, and continue cooking for another 45 minutes. *Serves 4.*

Pizza (illustrated on page 65)

Dough:
  1 cup flour
  1 level teaspoon salt
  ½ oz polyunsaturated margarine
  1 teaspoon dried yeast
  1 small teaspoon sugar
  ½ cup tepid water

8 oz canned tomatoes
¼ cup mushrooms
4 oz chicken or ham
4 oz cottage cheese
salt, pepper, paprika, mixed herbs

340 calories per serving
Sift flour and salt into a warm bowl. Rub margarine into flour. Cream yeast and sugar, mix with tepid water. Add to flour and beat thoroughly. Leave to rise for 20–30 minutes in a warm place till double in size. Divide the dough into two 8-in rounds; brush with oil. Chop mushrooms and sauté in minimum oil. Drain tomatoes. Finely chop chicken or ham. Mix cottage cheese, tomatoes, mushrooms, meat and seasonings together. Spread on rounds of dough and bake in a hot oven, 425°F, 220°C, till dough is risen and cooked, about 20 minutes. *Serves 4.*

Lentil rissoles

¼ cup lentils
¼ oz polyunsaturated margarine
1 small onion, finely chopped
1 cup water
salt, pepper
1 teaspoon ketchup
2 tablespoons farina
breadcrumbs for coating

Suitable for dieters: 200 calories per serving
Wash lentils. Melt margarine and sauté onion for a few minutes. Add lentils and toss. Add water, seasoning and ketchup. Simmer for about 1 hour till soft. Sprinkle in the farina and cook for 5 minutes, stirring well. Turn onto plate and cool. Shape into rolls or patties. Coat with breadcrumbs and fry till brown. *Serves 2.*

This is a useful recipe for vegetarians. It is also inexpensive and much more delicious than it actually sounds.

Suppertime kedgeree

½ cup rice
1 tablespoon cooking oil
1 hard-boiled egg white, chopped
6 oz cooked haddock
seasoning, ½ teaspoon curry powder
fresh chopped parsley or chives
½ cup cooked peas or corn

Suitable for dieters: 386 calories per serving
Cook rice. Flake fish. Place oil in pan. Add curry powder, egg white, rice, flaked fish, and peas or corn. Heat thoroughly. Mix in herbs, reserving some for garnish.   *Serves 2.*

Paella

6 tablespoons corn oil
1 onion, finely chopped
4 oz raw chicken, diced
¾ cup long grain rice
1 bouillon herb cube, dissolved in 1½ cups
    water
½ level teaspoon turmeric
¼ cup frozen peas
8-oz can tuna fish, flaked
1 red pepper, sliced

388 calories per serving
Heat oil and sauté onion and chicken for 5 minutes. Add rice and cook for further minute. Pour in mixed herb stock, and turmeric, peas, tuna and pepper. Bring to boil, cover tightly and simmer for 15 minutes until all liquid is absorbed.   *Serves 4.*

Snack patties

1 cup cooked meat
1 oz polyunsaturated margarine
1 onion, finely chopped
1 cup cold mashed potatoes
seasoning
½ teaspoon grated lemon rind
1 teaspoon chopped parsley
pinch nutmeg
skim milk and flour for coating
cooking oil

293 calories per serving
Chop meat finely. Melt margarine and sauté onion gently to soften. Mix with meat and potato. Add seasoning, lemon rind, parsley and nutmeg. Form into small flat cakes. Dip in milk and flour. Fry in oil until golden brown. Drain on paper towels to blot excess fat. Serve immediately with broiled tomatoes.   *Serves 4.*

Chicken crispies

½ cup savory white sauce:
  2 tablespoons flour
  1 oz polyunsaturated margarine
  ½ cup stock, made from bouillon cube or
  skim milk
1 cup chopped cooked chicken
seasoning
rolled oats for coating
cooking oil for frying

295 calories per serving
Make up sauce from flour, margarine and stock or milk. Stir in chicken and divide into four. Shape each portion into a pyramid. Coat in rolled oats. Heat oil to 375°F, 190°C, in deep pan. Sauté chicken for 2–3 minutes until golden brown. Serve hot or cold. *Serves 4.*

Mediterranean meatballs

1¼ lb ground lean beef
1 teaspoon lemon juice
grated rind of 1 medium lemon
4 tablespoons fine dry breadcrumbs
1 egg white
1 medium onion, finely chopped
1 teaspoon salt, freshly ground pepper
½ teaspoon mixed herbs
1 cup beef stock
small can tomato paste
2 teaspoons cornstarch
4 tablespoons cold water

217 calories per serving
Mix meat, lemon rind and juice, breadcrumbs, egg white, onion and seasonings. Add half stock. Mix again and leave to stand for 15 minutes. Form into six meatballs. Place on baking dish and bake at 350°F, 180°C, for 30 minutes. Make sauce by mixing remaining stock with tomato paste. Add seasoning. Mix cornstarch with cold water. Add to sauce. Bring to boil, stirring until smooth. Simmer for 5 minutes. Add to meatballs. Bake for further 15 minutes. *Serves 6.*

Fish fingers

12 oz thick haddock, cod or whiting fillets
cooking oil for frying
Batter:
  4 tablespoons flour
  4 tablespoons skim milk
  pinch salt or seasoned flour
skim milk
dried breadcrumbs

Fried: 156 calories per serving. Suitable for dieters if baked: 90 calories per serving
Cut fish into 3×1-in strips like fish fingers. If using batter, mix flour and skim milk together with salt. Dip fish into this and shallow fry in hot oil. Or dip fish in seasoned flour, milk and then breadcrumbs, and fry or bake in the oven at 350°F, 180°C, for 20 minutes. *Serves 4.*

Spaghetti Milanese

6 oz spaghetti
6 tablespoons cooking oil
1 onion, chopped
1 clove garlic, crushed
15-oz can peeled tomatoes
1 tablespoon tomato purée
2 mixed herb bouillon cubes
½ cup cooked ham, diced
¼ cup mushrooms, sliced

343 calories per serving
Cook spaghetti in boiling salted water until tender. Heat oil and sauté onion and garlic for 2–3 minutes. Add tomatoes, tomato purée and mixed herb cubes, bring to boil stirring. Add cooked ham and mushrooms, cover and simmer for 10 minutes. *Serves 4.*

Fast spaghetti

8 oz spaghetti
1 onion, peeled and chopped
1 clove garlic
2 tablespoons cooking oil
1½-lb can tomatoes
1 glass wine (optional)
1 can condensed consommé
8 tablespoons chopped cooked meat, if
    available
1 can corn, drained
1 bay leaf
mixed herbs and seasoning
few chopped olives

Without meat: 317 calories per serving.   With meat: 377 calories per serving
Cook spaghetti in plenty of boiling water. Meanwhile sauté onion and garlic gently in oil for 5 minutes. Add all the other ingredients, bring to boil and simmer until spaghetti is cooked. Drain and place on serving dish. Add the sauce. Garnish with chopped fresh herbs and a few chopped olives. *Serves 4.*

Chicken croquettes

1 cup ground chicken or turkey
½ cup thick white sauce:
    1 oz polyunsaturated margarine
    2 tablespoons flour
    ½ cup skim milk
½ teaspoon chopped parsley
2 tablespoons finely sliced mushrooms,
    sautéed in polyunsaturated margarine
1 teaspoon lemon juice (fresh or bottled)
2 tablespoons sherry (optional)

168 calories per serving
Mix all ingredients together. Form into rounds or sausage shapes. Roll in seasoned flour and dip in breadcrumbs, then in skim milk and again in breadcrumbs. Fry until golden brown in hot oil. Drain on paper towels. *Serves 4.*

Baked potato snack

1 large potato
2–4 tablespoons skim milk
½ oz polyunsaturated margarine
pinch pepper
¼ level teaspoon salt
2 tablespoons chopped parsley or finely
*   chopped cooked meats*
1 tablespoon chopped fried onion

248 calories
Scrub potato and brush skin with oil, or rub with greased paper. Place on baking shelf and cook until it feels soft when squeezed with a cloth. Cut in half lengthwise and scoop out the inside carefully. Mash this with milk, fat, seasonings and other chosen ingredients. Put back in the shell, brown in a hot oven for a few minutes, 400–425°F, 200–220°C.

Variations: 1. Fill with ground lean meat or flaked white fish. Moisten with a little fatless sauce and add chopped parsley. 2. Mix with skim milk, cottage cheese, and chopped green herbs.

Sardines on toast

4½-oz can sardines in oil
lemon juice
2 slices of toast

Suitable for dieters: 176 calories per serving
Drain sardines by putting in a wire sieve. Pour boiling water over them to remove excess oil. Mash into a soft paste with lemon juice. Spread on toast and place under the broiler to cook for a few moments.   *Serves 2.*

Sardine savories

pie dough:
*   ½ cup flour*
*   2 oz polyunsaturated margarine*
*   ¼ tablespoon baking powder*
4½-oz can sardines in oil
lemon juice

155 calories per serving
Make dough and roll out into a long strip. Drain sardines by putting in a wire sieve. Pour boiling water over them to remove excess oil. Mash with lemon juice. Spread on pastry strip and roll up like a jelly roll. Cut into circles and bake in a hot oven, 400°F, 200°C, for 10–15 minutes till lightly brown. A good party snack.   *Serves 8.*

Stuffed tomatoes (1)

4 large tomatoes
2–4 tablespoons fresh breadcrumbs
1 small onion, finely chopped
1 tablespoon chopped parsley, oregano or
    chervil
1 oz polyunsaturated margarine, melted
salt, pepper

160 calories per serving
Cut tops off tomatoes and reserve lids. Scoop centers into a bowl. Add crumbs, onion, herbs, margarine and seasoning and mix well. Pile back into tomato cases and put lids back on. Place in greased dish and heat in a fairly hot oven at 400°F, 200°C, for 15 minutes.   *Serves 2.*

Variations: 1. Use $\frac{1}{4}$ cup chopped lobster instead of onion. 2. Use $\frac{1}{4}$ cup cooked lean lamb, finely chopped.

Stuffed tomatoes (2)

6 medium-sized firm tomatoes

Filling:
    $\frac{1}{2}$ oz polyunsaturated margarine
    1 teaspoon chopped onion
    2–3 fresh mushrooms, chopped
    $\frac{1}{4}$ cup chopped cooked chicken
    4 tablespoons white breadcrumbs
    a little sauce or tomato pulp
    pinch ground mace, cayenne, salt
    dried breadcrumbs

Suitable for dieters: 123 calories per serving
Wipe the tomatoes and cut a small round from each at the end opposite the stalk. Scoop out all the pulp from the inside and turn cases upside down for a short time to drain. Melt polyunsaturated margarine in a frying pan and sauté onion and mushrooms until cooked. Add chicken and other ingredients, making the mixture rather soft. Fill tomatoes with this, sprinkle with breadcrumbs and bake in a moderate oven, 350°F, 180°C, for 12–15 minutes.   *Serves 3.*

Ledsham tomatoes

4 large tomatoes
1 teaspoon dry mustard
$\frac{1}{4}$ cup lean cooked ham
2 oz cottage cheese
seasoning, paprika
chopped chives
little brown sugar (optional)

Suitable for dieters: 119 calories per serving
Slice tops from tomatoes. Scoop out insides into bowl, separating juice from flesh. Mix 1 teaspoon dry mustard with tomato juice. Chop ham; add to tomato flesh and mustard. Add cheese. Mix and season to taste. Add chopped chives and fill tomatoes liberally. Place in baking dish. Add pinch brown sugar to top of each tomato. Bake at 350°F, 180°C, for 15–20 minutes till tops are brown. Serve hot.   *Serves 2.*

Spinach soufflé

$\frac{1}{2}$ cup spinach purée
$\frac{3}{4}$ oz polyunsaturated margarine
$1\frac{1}{2}$ tablespoons flour
salt, pepper
3 tablespoons skim milk powder
2 egg whites

Suitable for dieters: 220 calories per serving
Mix spinach purée, flour and margarine. Add seasonings and skim milk powder. Cool slightly. Fold in stiffly beaten egg whites. Turn into a greased fireproof dish and bake in a moderately hot oven, 350°F, 180°C, for 30–40 minutes, till well risen and firm to touch. Serve immediately. *Serves 2–3.*

Savory soufflé

$1\frac{1}{2}$ tablespoons flour
$\frac{3}{4}$ oz polyunsaturated margarine
$\frac{1}{2}$ cup skim milk
$\frac{1}{3}$ cup ground cooked meat, e.g. ham or
    chicken
salt, pepper
2 egg whites

Suitable for dieters: 245 calories per serving
Mix fat, flour, and skim milk. Stir in ground meat and add seasoning. Fold in stiffly beaten egg whites and turn into a greased fireproof dish. Bake in a moderately hot oven, 350°F, 180°C, for 30 minutes, till well risen and firm to the touch. Serve immediately. *Serves 2–3.*

Quick risotto

1 cup uncooked rice
thyme
bay leaf
clove
1 onion, diced
4 tablespoons cooking oil
1½ cups pre-cooked diced lean meat

About 287 calories per serving
Cook rice in boiling water with thyme, bay leaf and clove. Sauté onion in oil, add rice and brown slightly. Add meat and heat through. Serve with peas or green beans. *Serves 4.*

Cottager's ham

4 tablespoons cooking oil
½ cup onions, chopped
1 large package frozen peas
½ cup water
salt and pepper
¼ cup lean ham, chopped

Suitable for dieters: 129 calories per serving
Heat oil and sauté onions without browning for 5 minutes. Add peas, water, salt and pepper, simmer for 5 minutes. Add ham, cover and simmer for 10 minutes. ¼ (cup ham is sufficient only to flavor peas. More may be added if required.) *Serves 4.*

Tripe and onions

1 lb prepared tripe
2 cups skim milk (hot)
8 oz onions
salt and pepper
1 oz polyunsaturated margarine
2 tablespoons flour

262 calories per serving
Cut tripe into strips about 3 × 1½ in. Place in a casserole with sliced onions, salt, pepper and hot skim milk. Cook for 1 hour in a moderate oven, 325°F, 160°C. When cooked, make a sauce by melting margarine in a pan, adding flour and cooking very slowly till it forms a roux but does not brown. Gradually add the milk stock from the tripe and bring to boil, stirring all the time. Simmer for 3–5 minutes. Pour over tripe and serve with toast. *Serves 4.*
Use only occasionally.

Dieters' rarebit

½ oz polyunsaturated margarine
1 tablespoon flour
6 tablespoons skim milk
salt and pepper
4 oz cottage cheese
1 teaspoon prepared mustard
dash Worcestershire sauce
pinch cayenne
2 tablespoons beer if available

Suitable for dieters: 146 calories per serving
Melt margarine, add flour and then milk. Cook thoroughly. Beat in the seasoning, cheese, mustard, Worcestershire sauce, cayenne and beer. Pour over hot toast.   *Serves 2.*

Cottage cheese and ham rarebit

4 thick slices bread
8 oz cottage cheese
¼ cup lean chopped ham
salt, pepper
1 teaspoon prepared mustard

406 calories per serving
Cut crusts from bread and toast on one side. On untoasted side spread mixture of cottage cheese, ham and seasonings. Place under hot broiler and cook until cheese begins to bubble. Serve immediately.   *Serves 2–4.*

Toast toppers

1 slice white or brown bread

Mushroom topping (per person):
  2 small mushrooms, finely chopped
  1 small tomato, finely chopped
  2 tablespoons sweet pickle

Fish topping (per person):
  4 tablespoons tuna fish, drained and flaked
  1 teaspoon lemon juice

Suitable for dieters: With mushrooms: 136 calories.   With fish: 210 calories
Toast one side of bread. Mix topping well together and spread evenly on untoasted side of bread. Replace under broiler for a few minutes to brown.

Sandwich fillings with cooked meats

Beef:
    +*mustard*
    +*pickle*
    +*chopped scallion*
    +*tomato*
Chicken:
    +*watercress*
    +*cottage cheese*
    +*salad vegetables*
    +*dill pickles*
Ham:
    +*dill pickles*
    +*tomato ketchup*
    +*cottage cheese and chives*
Pork:
    +*grated apple and lemon juice*
    +*mango chutney*

These can be prepared in advance, foil-wrapped and stored in a home freezer to save time when meals are taken to work or school and picnics prepared. If taken out before work a package will be thawed in time for lunch.

Toasted sandwiches

Chopped cooked chicken and special
    mayonnaise (page 68)
Chopped ham and French mustard
Crispy bacon and ketchup
Eggless lemon spread
Mushrooms, fried in oil
Cooking oil, brown sugar and cinnamon

Toast bread on one side. Spread filling on untoasted side, then heat under broiler. Serve very hot.

Cottage cheese fillings

Chopped chives	*Parsley*
Scallions	*Mint*
Dill pickle	*Dill*
Watercress	*Sliced radishes*
Celery	*Pineapple*
Tomato	*Lettuce*
Cucumber	*Walnuts*

Combine cottage cheese with any of these fillings for variety of flavor.

Sandwich fillings with fish

Sardines (drained of olive oil)
Smoked cod or haddock
White flaked fish
Kipper
Anchovies
Salmon
Tuna
Herring

Combine with a savory sauce or vinegar to make moist and easy to spread.

Sandwich fillings with vegetables

Celery
Chives
Watercress
Scallions
Cucumber
Lettuce
Tomato
Beets
Chicory
Onion
Mustard and cress
Radishes
Grated carrot
Fried mushrooms
Dill pickles
Crushed corn (canned)
Parsley
Mint
String beans

Calorie value depends upon filling chosen.

Vegetables may be chopped and combined using special low-cholesterol mayonnaise (page 68) or other low animal fat sauces to bind them. Chopped fruits, nuts, cottage cheese and hard-boiled egg white also mix well with some vegetables.

Sandwich fillings with fruit

Banana, mashed
  +lemon juice and brown sugar
Apple, grated
  +celery, beets and special mayonnaise (page 68)
  +celery, walnuts and special mayonnaise (page 68)
  +dates or raisins
Dates, mashed
  +lemon or orange juice
  +lemon juice and apple
  +lemon juice and nuts
Raisins, chopped
  +honey and lemon juice
  +grated apple
Pineapple, crushed
  +cottage cheese

Use polyunsaturated margarine to spread on bread, preferably brown bread, which enhances the flavor of the fruit.

Hot bread

Vienna loaf + one of the flavored "butters"
below

Slice the loaf in half lengthwise. Spread the flavored margarine generously along the cut sides and sandwich the bread back together. Wrap the bread in foil and place in a hot oven, 400°F, 200°C, for approximately 7 minutes. Serve the hot bread with soups, stews and casseroles.

Garlic "butter"

2 cloves garlic
2 oz polyunsaturated margarine

445 calories
Peel the garlic cloves and blanch in boiling water for 3 minutes. Drain and chop very finely. Cream the margarine and beat in garlic.

Mixed herb "butter"

2 oz polyunsaturated margarine
1 teaspoon dried mixed herbs
1 teaspoon lemon juice

445 calories
Cream the margarine and beat in the herbs and lemon juice.

Paprika "butter"

2 oz polyunsaturated margarine
1 teaspoon paprika
pinch salt

445 calories
Cream the margarine and beat in the paprika and salt.

Baking

This diet does mean that bought cakes are on the banned list because you can't be sure they contain the right ingredients. The baking recipes are designed to lure you away from the bakery and into the kitchen to whip up your own selection of crisp breads and delicious cakes or cookies. Home baking makes more economic sense than buying cakes. Also there is nothing quite as special as the flavor of homemade cakes. These recipes concentrate on cookies and cakes that do not need the addition of butter and egg yolks. It is worth remembering though, that polyunsaturated margarine can always be substituted for butter for home-baked cakes.

Bran loaf

1 cup whole wheat flour
1 cup flour
½ cup bran
2 teaspoons salt
2 tablespoons oil
Yeast liquid:
  1 teaspoon sugar
  1½ cups warm water
  3 teaspoons dried yeast

1020 calories per loaf

Place flours, bran and salt in bowl. Add oil and frothy yeast liquid; mix to firm dough. Turn onto a lightly floured surface and knead well for 5 minutes. Place in oiled plastic bag and leave to rise in a warm place for about 1 to 1½ hours. Turn risen dough out onto floured surface and flatten with knuckles. Divide into two. Shape to fit two oiled 1-lb loaf pans. Brush tops with salt water and place in oiled plastic bags. Leave in warm place until double in size. Bake at 450°F, 230°C, for about 45 minutes or until the loaves sound hollow when tapped. *Makes 2 loaves.*

White plait (illustrated on page 111)

3 cups flour
2 teaspoons salt
1 teaspoon sugar
½ oz polyunsaturated margarine

Yeast liquid:
  1 teaspoon sugar
  2 cups warm water
  3 teaspoons dried yeast

2515 calories

Rub margarine into flour, salt and sugar. Pour in yeast liquid and form into firm dough. Turn onto lightly floured surface; knead for 10 minutes. Divide in half. For each half: cut into 3 pieces, roll pieces into strands, plait together and pinch ends. Brush with skim milk and sprinkle with poppy seeds. Place on oiled tray and cover with plastic bag. Leave to rise in warm place until double in size. Bake in hot oven, 450°F, 230°C, for about 30–35 minutes.

French onion bread (illustrated opposite)

2 cups flour
½ teaspoon salt
2 tablespoons sugar
2 tablespoons oil
3 tablespoons French onion soup mix
¾ cup water
Yeast liquid:
    1 teaspoon sugar
    ½ cup warm water
    2 teaspoons dried yeast

963 calories per loaf
Place flour, salt and sugar in bowl. Combine oil, soup mix and water; bring to boil and simmer for 10 minutes. Cool and add to flour with yeast liquid. Mix to firm dough, turn onto floured surface and knead until smooth. Place in oiled plastic bag and leave in warm place to rise until double, about 1 hour. Turn dough onto floured surface and flatten with knuckles. Divide into two. Shape pieces into ovals. Place on floured baking sheet. With sharp knife make diagonal cuts on top, about ⅛-in deep and 1 in apart. Brush with a little beaten egg white, cover with plastic wrap. Allow to rise until almost double in size, about 30 minutes. Bake at 375°F, 190°C, about 25 minutes or until crisp and brown.   *Makes 2 small loaves.*

Whole wheat rolls (illustrated opposite)

2 cups whole wheat flour
1 teaspoon salt
1 teaspoon sugar
2 tablespoons cooking oil

Yeast liquid:
    1 teaspoon sugar
    1 cup warm water
    2 tablespoons dried yeast

139 calories per roll
Dissolve sugar in warm water and sprinkle on dried yeast. Leave until frothy – about 10 minutes. Mix together flour, salt, sugar, oil and yeast liquid to form a dough. Turn onto floured surface and knead until smooth and no longer sticky, about 4 minutes. Place dough in oiled plastic bag and leave in warm place until double in size, about 1 hour. Turn dough onto floured surface and flatten with knuckles. Divide dough into 12 pieces and shape into small balls. Place on floured baking sheets. Cut a cross on top for decoration. Cover with plastic wrap and allow to rise in warm place until almost double in size, about 20–30 minutes. Bake at 450°F, 230°C, for about 20 minutes or until golden brown and crisp. *Makes 12.*

Tea loaf (illustrated opposite)

1¼ cup flour
1 rounded teaspoon baking soda
½ rounded teaspoon cream of tartar
pinch salt
6 tablespoons sugar
4 oz polyunsaturated margarine
½ cup white raisins
¼ cup chopped walnuts
skim milk to mix

2968 calories
Mix dry ingredients, rub in margarine and add fruit and nuts. Add milk until mixture is of "dropping" consistency. Bake in greased and lined loaf pan for about 1 hour in a moderate oven, 350°F, 180°C, until loaf is light brown and springy to touch and beginning to leave sides of tin. White raisins and walnuts can be substituted with: ½ cup chopped dates, ½ cup white raisins, using only ¼ cup sugar or ½ cup each of white raisins and currants with a little mixed peel or 1 cup dates or 1 cup crystallized ginger.

Fruit cake (illustrated opposite)

4 oz polyunsaturated margarine
1 cup sugar
2 cups flour
1 tablespoon baking soda
pinch salt
½ cup currants
1 cup mixed seedless and white raisins
2 tablespoons peel
8 tablespoons skim milk
½ wine glass vinegar

4667 calories
Melt margarine and sugar together. Mix into flour very slowly. Stir in other ingredients slowly. Add vinegar last. Put in prepared cake pan, place in a moderate oven, 350°F, 180°C, and bake for 1½ hours. Size of cake pan to use: $11 \times 9 \times 1\frac{1}{2}$in.

Orange feather cake (illustrated opposite)

4 oz polyunsaturated margarine
½ cup sugar
rind of 1 orange
5 egg whites, stiffly beaten
½ cup flour, sifted with 1 teaspoon baking
  powder

Orange icing:
  3 oz polyunsaturated margarine
  1 cup confectioners' sugar
  4 tablespoons orange juice

3486 calories
Cream margarine and sugar together until light and fluffy. Stir in orange rind. Fold in egg whites and flour alternately. Place in greased and floured 7-in cake pan. Bake at 350°F, 180°C, for 30–40 minutes until firm.

Icing: Place all ingredients in mixing bowl and beat together with wooden spoon until smooth. Split cake in half and sandwich two halves together with half orange icing. Spread remaining icing over top of cake. Pipe rosettes round edge if desired.

This mixture also makes a good sponge pudding.

Lightning fruit cake

2 cups self-rising flour
1 cup soft brown sugar
4 cups mixed dried fruit
1½ cups cooking oil
2 beaten egg whites
1 cup boiling skim milk

6275 calories
Line a 9-in round cake pan with waxed paper. Sift flour and mix in sugar and dried fruit. Stir in oil and egg whites. Stir in boiling milk and mix well. Turn into the prepared pan and bake on low shelf in oven, 350°F, 180°C, for 1¾–2 hours. This cake should be kept for one week before cutting.

Wartime fruit cake

½ cup syrup
½ cup white raisins
½ cup currants
½ cup skim milk
1 teaspoon mixed spice
pinch salt
4 oz polyunsaturated margarine
1½ cups sifted flour
½ teaspoon baking powder
1 teaspoon baking soda
2 tablespoons warm water

3841 calories
Boil together in a saucepan for 3 minutes the syrup, white raisins, currants, skim milk, mixed spice, salt and margarine. Place flour in bowl. Add baking powder. When ingredients in saucepan are cold add baking soda dissolved in warm water. Then add these ingredients to flour in bowl. Mix thoroughly, place in lined and greased cake pan and bake in moderate oven for 1½–2 hours at 350°F, 180°C. Size of pan to use: 11 × 9 × 1½ in.

Belgian fruit cake

1 cup currants and white raisins, mixed
4 oz polyunsaturated margarine
1 cup sugar
1 cup cold tea
2 cups flour
pinch salt
3 level teaspoons baking powder
1 level teaspoon baking soda
1 level teaspoon mixed spice

3255 calories
Put fruit, margarine, sugar and cold tea in saucepan, set over low heat, bring to boil and boil gently for 10 minutes, then draw pan aside to cool. Sift together flour, salt, baking powder, soda and spice. Make well in middle of flour, add boiled fruit mixture and mix well together to make soft dough. Put into greased, lined cake pan. Bake 1½ hours at 350°F, 180°C. Size of pan to use: 11 × 9 × 1½ in.

Gingerbread

1¼ cups flour
1 teaspoon baking soda
1½ teaspoons ground ginger
½ teaspoon salt
½ cup boiling water
4 oz polyunsaturated margarine
1½ cups molasses or syrup
dried fruit may be added if desired

3225 calories
Sift dry ingredients; melt margarine in boiling water, add syrup. Add dry ingredients and mix well. Grease 8-in loaf pan, bake in moderate oven, 375°F, 190°C, for 40–50 minutes.

Sticky gingerbread

1½ cups cooking oil
2 cups dark molasses
3 cups flour
1 cup sugar
½ teaspoon salt
1 teaspoon ground ginger
½ cup skim milk
1 teaspoon baking soda

6479 calories
Brush load pan approximately 9½ × 7½ × 2½ in with oil and line base with waxed paper. Warm oil and molasses. Sift flour, salt, sugar and ground ginger together. Warm milk and stir baking soda into it. Stir warm oil and molasses into dry ingredients and then add milk and soda. Beat thoroughly. Turn into prepared pan and bake for approximately 2 hours at 325°F, 160°C.

Ginger-coffee crunch cake

4 oz polyunsaturated margarine
4 tablespoons syrup
1 tablespoon sugar
1 teaspoon ground ginger
1 cup arrowroot cookies

Coffee icing:
* 3 oz polyunsaturated margarine*
* 1 cup sifted confectioners' sugar*
* 4 tablespoons strong black coffee or 2*
* tablespoons coffee extract*

2673 calories
Place margarine, syrup, sugar and ginger in saucepan and melt gently. Crush cookies and mix. Spread mixture in prepared cake pan $9 \times 9 \times 1\frac{1}{2}$ in. Allow to set and top with coffee icing. To make coffee icing: place all ingredients in a bowl, beat until smooth and then spread over cake.

Quick white cake

1 cup sifted flour
1 teaspoon salt
1 cup sugar
8 tablespoons cooking oil
1 cup skim milk
3 teaspoons baking powder
4 egg whites
1 teaspoon vanilla

4697 calories
Prepare two 8-in cake pans by greasing lightly with oil or polyunsaturated margarine and dusting with flour. Sift together in mixing bowl the flour, salt and sugar. Add oil and $\frac{3}{4}$ cup of milk. Stir until flour is dampened and beat for one minute. Stir in baking powder and add remaining milk, egg whites and vanilla. Beat 2 minutes. Pour into cake pans and bake 25–40 minutes, 350°F, 180°C. These cakes may be filled with jelly and iced on top.

Angel cake

6 tablespoons flour
pinch of salt
$\frac{1}{2}$ teaspoon cream of tartar
1 teaspoon baking powder
6 tablespoons cornstarch
1 cup sugar
skim milk to mix (about $\frac{1}{2}$ cup)
flavoring: vanilla, orange, lemon, etc.
3 egg whites

1588 calories
Sift dry ingredients, stir in sugar. Mix with milk and add flavoring. Beat egg whites until stiff and fold in. Pour into deep, ungreased tin. Bake for about 50 minutes at 370°F, 190°C.

Spiced apple cake

$1\frac{1}{4}$ cup flour
3 teaspoons baking powder
2 tablespoons sugar
$\frac{3}{4}$ teaspoon salt
6 oz polyunsaturated margarine
$\frac{3}{4}$ cup skim milk

Topping:
   2–3 apples
   $\frac{1}{2}$ teaspoon cinnamon
   2 tablespoons brown sugar
   $1\frac{1}{2}$ oz polyunsaturated margarine

3090 calories
Sift flour, white sugar, baking powder and salt. Rub in margarine roughly. Add milk to make soft dough. Put into ungreased 9-in cake pan. Peel, core and slice apples, arrange on top of dough. Sprinkle with brown sugar and cinnamon and dot with margarine. Bake in hot oven 30–40 minutes at 440°F, 230°C.

Tyrol cake

$3\frac{1}{2}$ oz polyunsaturated margarine
1 cup flour
1 level teaspoon ground cinnamon
4 tablespoons sugar
4 tablespoons currants
4 tablespoons white raisins
1 level teaspoon baking soda
$\frac{1}{2}$ cup skim milk
4 tablespoons clear honey

2456 calories
Grease and flour 6-in cake pan. Rub fat into flour and cinnamon until mixture resembles fine breadcrumbs. Stir in sugar and fruit and make well in center. Dissolve baking soda in some of the milk, add to honey and pour into well. Gradually work in dry ingredients, adding more milk if necessary to give dropping consistency. Put into the pan and level the top. Bake in center of warm oven, 325°F, 160°C, for $1\frac{3}{4}$–2 hours until well risen and firm.

Donut rings

$\frac{3}{4}$ cup flour
1 level teaspoon baking powder
pinch salt
pinch nutmeg
4 tablespoons sugar
2 tablespoons cooking oil
2 egg whites
4 tablespoons skim milk

178 calories per donut
Sift all dry ingredients together into mixing bowl. Mix together oil, egg whites and milk and add to dry ingredients. Knead lightly on floured board. Roll out to $\frac{1}{4}$-in thickness and cut into 6 rounds with plain $2\frac{1}{2}$-in cutter, then remove round from center of each with smaller cutter to form ring. Heat oil to 360°F, 185°C, and sauté, turning frequently, until golden brown on both sides. Drain and sprinkle thickly with sugar. *Makes 6.*

Cherry buns

¾ cup self-rising flour
⅓ cup candied cherries
2 egg whites
3 oz polyunsaturated margarine
½ cup sugar
8 tablespoons skim milk
grated rind of ½ lemon

90 calories per bun
Sift flour, cut cherries in quarters, beat egg whites to stiff froth. Beat margarine and sugar to very soft cream; then gradually stir in milk. Add beaten egg whites. Now stir in flour and lemon rind. When quite smooth add cherries, first dusting them in a little flour to prevent them sinking in buns. Fill patty tins three-quarters full with mixture and bake at once in hot oven, 450°F, 230°C, for about 20 minutes.   *Makes 24.*

Plain scones

1 cup flour
½ teaspoon salt
2 teaspoons baking powder
3 tablespoons cooking oil
skim milk to mix

162 calories per scone
Mix all ingredients together. Use milk to get a soft, but not wet, consistency. Roll out ½-in thick on floured board. Cut in 8 rounds and bake in a hot oven, 440°F, 230°C, for 15 minutes.
Makes 8.

Raisin scones

1 cup self-rising flour
1 level teaspoon cream of tartar
½ level teaspoon soda
or 1½ teaspoons baking powder
4 tablespoons white raisins
2 tablespoons sugar
skim milk to mix
3 tablespoons cooking oil

192 calories per scone
Mix all ingredients together. Use skim milk to get a soft, but not wet, consistency. Roll out ½-in thick on floured board. Cut in 8 rounds and bake in a hot oven, 440°F, 230°C, for 15 minutes.
Makes 8.

Basic cookies

½ cup sugar
6 tablespoons cooking oil
¾ cup flour
pinch of salt
dried fruit and nuts (optional)
flavoring: vanilla, almond, orange rind, etc.

255 calories per cookie
Mix all ingredients. Roll out and shape. Bake 15–20 minutes, 370°F, 190°C.   *Makes 8.*

Plain cookies

1 cup sifted flour
3 teaspoons baking powder
½ teaspoon salt
4 tablespoons cooking oil
¾ cup skim milk

184 calories per cookie
Sift flour, baking powder and salt together into mixing bowl. Pour oil and milk into measuring cup, but do not sir. Add all at once to flour mixture. Stir quickly with fork until dough clings together. Knead dough lightly about 10 times. Pat dough out to about ½-in thick. Cut 12 rounds with unfloured medium-size cutter. Place cookies on ungreased baking sheet and bake for 12–15 minutes at 475°F, 240°C.   *Makes 12.*

Crackers

½ cup flour
2 tablespoons cooking oil
3 tablespoons (approx.) water

84 calories per cracker
Mix all ingredients. Roll out thinly and prick. Bake for 15 minutes at 415°F, 210°C.   *Makes 12.*

Nut crisps

4 oz polyunsaturated margarine
6 tablespoons sugar
4 tablespoons honey or maple syrup
$\frac{2}{3}$ cup flour
$\frac{1}{4}$ cup walnuts
$\frac{1}{2}$ teaspoon baking powder
1 teaspoon ground ginger
vanilla extract

226 calories per crisp
Cream margarine and sugar. Add syrup, then mix in dry ingredients, flavoring and chopped walnuts. Shape into 12 small rounds and flatten. Bake on a greased tray in a moderate oven, 350°F, 180°C, for 10–15 minutes.   *Makes 12.*

Molasses cake

Yeast liquid:
    1 teaspoon sugar
    $\frac{3}{4}$ cup warm water
    3 teaspoons dried yeast
1 cup whole wheat flour
1 cup flour
2 teaspoons salt
1 oz polyunsaturated margarine
6 tablespoons dark molasses
$\frac{1}{2}$ cup raisins

1943 calories
Dissolve sugar in warm water and sprinkle on yeast. Leave until frothy – about 10 minutes. Place flours and salt in a bowl and rub in margarine. Blend molasses with yeast liquid. Add to flour. Mix to firm dough. Turn on to lightly floured surface and knead for 5 minutes. Place dough in an oiled plastic bag and leave to prove for 1–1$\frac{1}{2}$ hours until double in size. Turn dough on to a floured surface and work in raisins until evenly distributed. Shape dough to fit a 2-lb loaf tin. Place in oiled cake pan, cover with plastic wrap and leave in a warm place until almost double in size, about 50 minutes. Bake at 450°F, 230°C, for 45 minutes or until loaf sounds hollow when tapped.

Rum crunchies

3 oz polyunsaturated margarine
6 tablespoons sugar
1 egg white, large
$\frac{3}{4}$ teaspoon rum extract
or 2 tablespoons Jamaica rum
6 tablespoons flour, sifted
candied cherries to decorate, sugar to
    sprinkle

72 calories per crunchie
Cream margarine and sugar together until light and fluffy. Add egg white and beat the mixture until thick and creamy (3–4 minutes). Add rum extract, or rum, then stir in flour. Place teaspoonsful of mixture well apart on lightly greased baking sheet. Press half a candied cherry into each. Bake on middle shelf of oven, 350°F, 180°C, for 10–15 minutes. Cool on wire tray, then dredge with sugar.   *Makes 19–20.*

Nutty meringues

1 egg white
½ cup sugar
¼ teaspoon salt
½ teaspoon vanilla extract
½ cup chopped walnuts
½ cup cornflakes

60 calories per meringue
Beat egg white in large bowl. Beat in sugar gradually. Beat in salt and vanilla. Fold in walnuts and cornflakes. Take up heaped teaspoonsful of mixture and push with another teaspoon onto well-oiled baking sheet. Bake at 300°F, 150°C, for about 20 minutes or until surface is dry but not brown. Remove from sheet with a knife while still warm. *Makes 24.*

Oat crisps

1¼ cups rolled oats
1¼ cups flour
½ teaspoon baking powder
½ teaspoon salt
6 oz polyunsaturated margarine
¼ cup brown sugar
½ cup water

Filling:
  ¾ cup raisins
  ¼ cup sugar
  1 oz polyunsaturated margarine

467 calories per crisp
Sift flour, salt and baking powder, and add oats. Cream margarine and sugar. Add dry ingredients alternately with water. Chill. Roll out to ½-in thickness and cut into 12 rounds. Bake on greased cookie sheet in moderate ove, 350°F, 180°C, for 10 minutes. Allow to cool. Meanwhile make filling. Heat filling ingredients gently in pan. Allow to cool, then use as sandwich filling between the cookies. *Makes 12.*

Fruity almond squares

2 egg whites
½ cup confectioner's sugar
6 tablespoons self-rising flour
½ teaspoon salt
¼ cup ground almonds
few drops almond extract
6 tablespoons cooking oil
½ cup stoned dates, chopped
½ cup mixed citrus peel

158 calories per square
Brush shallow pan approximately 8-in square or 10×6-in oblong with oil. Whip the egg whites slightly then beat in the sugar ¼ cup at a time until mixture thickens. Sift flour and salt together. Gradually fold into egg-white mixture with ground almonds, almond extract and oil. Fold in dates and mixed citrus peel. Turn into a prepared pan and bake at 325°F, 160°C, for 35 minutes. Cut into 16 squares while still warm. Allow to cool before removing from the pan. *Makes 16.*

Butterscotch fingers

1 cup flour
¼ teaspoon salt
¾ cup soft brown sugar
¾ cup cooking oil
1 egg white
1 teaspoon vanilla extract

Topping:
  ¾ cup butterscotch candies
  3 tablespoons cooking oil
  2 tablespoons water
  ¼ teaspoon salt

159 calories per finger
To make topping, place butterscotch candies in oil, water and salt in a bowl over boiling water and melt gradually; this will take approximately 45 minutes. Brush shallow pan, approximately 12×7×1 in, with oil. Sift flour and salt together and mix in sugar. Stir in oil, egg white and vanilla extract; mix well together. Turn into prepared pan and bake at 350°F, 180°C, for 20 minutes. Allow to cool slightly, then spread topping over cake. Allow the topping to set, then cut into fingers. *Makes 20.*

Shortbread

½ cup flour
¼ cup flour
¼ cup sugar
4 oz polyunsaturated margarine

224 calories per square
Rub margarine into flour and sugar. Knead well. Roll out ⅛-in thick, prick well. Cut out 8 squares and bake in cool oven, 300°F, 150°C, for 20 minutes. *Makes 8.*

Shortcake

⅓ cup flour
2 tablespoons cornstarch
4 tablespoons sugar
2 tablespoons confectioner's sugar
8 tablespoons cooking oil

2236 calories
Sift flour and cornstarch. Add sugar, stir in oil. Press into greased shallow pan and bake for 1 hour at 440°F, 230°C.

Ginger crunch

4 oz polyunsaturated margarine
½ cup sugar
¾ cup flour
½ teaspoon baking powder
½ teaspoon ground ginger

Icing:
  ½ cup confectioner's sugar
  3 teaspoons honey or maple syrup
  1 oz polyunsaturated margarine
  1 teaspoon ground ginger

239 calories per crunch
Cream margarine and sugar and add sifted dry ingredients. Press mixture into thin layer in a shallow greased tin and bake for 20–30 minutes in a moderate oven, 350°F, 180°C.

Icing: heat all ingredients together in pan until they are melted and beat thoroughly. Pour icing over crunch while both are still warm. Cut into 12 squares before completely cold.   *Makes 12.*

Brandy snaps

2 level tablespoons honey or maple syrup
2 oz polyunsaturated margarine
3 tablespoons sugar
3 tablespoons flour, sifted
½ level teaspoon ground ginger

102 calories per snap
Grease two large baking sheets. Put honey or syrup, margarine and sugar into heavy-based saucepan. Heat gently until all ingredients have dissolved. Remove from heat, beat in flour and ginger until smooth. Drop teaspoons of mixture 2 in apart, on prepared baking sheets. Bake in two batches, in center of pre-heated oven, 400°F, 200°C, for 5–6 minutes each, or until golden brown. Meanwhile grease handle of wooden spoon. Leave snaps to cool very slightly on baking sheet. Remove carefully with palette knife and wrap each one round handle of wooden spoon. Remove, and put on wire rack to finish cooling. Store in airtight tin.   *Makes 10.*

Oatmeal fingers

6 oz polyunsaturated margarine
4 tablespoons soft brown sugar
6 tablespoons honey or maple syrup
1½ cups rolled oats
¼ level teaspoon salt

233 calories per finger
Grease a 7×11-in jelly roll pan with oil. Put margarine and sugar in mixing bowl. Beat well until soft and fluffy. Heat syrup gently in small saucepan. Beat into creamed mixture. Beat in oats and salt. Spread mixture in prepared pan and bake in the center of a pre-heated oven, 400°F, 200°C, for 30 minutes or until golden brown. While mixture is still hot, cut into fingers but leave in tin to complete cooling; remove very carefully.
Makes 14.

Eating Guide

Use this guide as a handy reference when selecting food. People already under the care of their doctor and dietitian should check first. The guide can then be approved and used as an adjunct to their existing eating pattern.

1 For people who don't need to watch their weight

However, it is still important not to get overweight by eating too much.

Low-fat, low-saturated fat, low-cholesterol diet. No calorie limit.

Daily allowance: 2 cups skim milk – more if desired.
low-fat natural yogurt as desired.
2–3 tablespoons oil – safflower, sunflower, corn, soya bean.
1 oz polyunsaturated margarine.

Weekly allowance: 1 whole egg.

Allowed
Dairy products: Skim milk, low-fat yogurt, egg white, plain ice cream, cottage cheese.
Fats: Polyunsaturated margarine, oils – safflower, sunflower, corn, soya bean.
Meat, poultry, fish: Small portions of lean meat, i.e. beef, lamb, pork, ham, bacon. Medium portions of chicken, rabbit, turkey, veal. Large portions of white fish, smoked haddock.
Soup: Clear soups, i.e. consommé, broths, purée or cream soups made using oil or polyunsaturated margarine.
Cereals: All breakfast and desserts, pastas.
Breads, pastries, cookies: Any prepared with suitable fat or egg white.
Desserts: Any prepared with skim milk or suitable fats. Meringues (no cream), jellos, sherberts.
Vegetables and fruit: All (fresh, frozen, canned, dried). Potatoes to be cooked in suitable margarine or oil.
Miscellaneous: Tea, coffee, soft drinks, minerals, salt, pepper, herbs, spices. In moderation sugar, jelly, marmalade, honey, boiled candies, walnuts. almonds.

Forbidden
Dairy products: Whole milk, including evaporated, full cream dried. Cream, imitation cream, coffee creamers, sour cream, butter, other cheeses, whole egg, egg yolk, dairy or fancy ice creams.
Fats: Other margarines, lard, dripping, suet, cooking fats, meat fats, coconut and palm oil.
Meat, poultry, fish: All fatty meats, sausages, fatty cold meats, i.e. salami, luncheon meat, goose, duck, game and high-cholesterol meats and fish.
Soup: Greasy soups, soups except those made with polyunsaturated oil and margarine. *Watch* canned and packaged varieties.
Cereals: Egg noodles.
Breads, pastries, cookies: Those prepared with forbidden fats or egg yolks. Donuts, cream cakes, bought cakes and cookies, including cake mixes.
Desserts: Those prepared with forbidden fats or egg yolks. Pancakes, suet pudding, bought pastries.
Vegetables: Potato chips, potatoes cooked in forbidden fats. *Watch* bought chips or when eating out.
Miscellaneous: Mayonnaise, salad dressing, malted milk drinks, chocolate, cashew nuts, coconut.

2 For dieters

Low-calorie, low-fat, low-saturated fat, low-cholesterol diet.
1,500 calorie limit.

Daily allowance: 2 cups skim milk or $1\frac{1}{2}$ cups skim milk plus $\frac{2}{3}$ cup low-fat natural yogurt.
1 tablespoon oil – safflower, sunflower, corn, soya bean.
$\frac{1}{2}$ oz polyunsaturated margarine.
7 portions from the Bread Exchange List, *see* page 125.

Weekly allowance: 1 whole egg.

Allowed
Dairy products: Skim milk and low-fat natural yogurt allowance.
Fats: Polyunsaturated margarine, oil allowance.
Meat, poultry, fish: Small portions of lean meat. Medium portions of chicken, turkey, rabbit, veal. Large portions of white fish, smoked haddock.

Soups: Clear soups, broths and unthickened purée soups.

Breads, cereals: 7 portions from the Bread Exchange List, *see* below.

Vegetables: Potatoes boiled, mashed or in the jacket, and dried vegetables from allowance. Salads, green vegetables (fresh, frozen, canned), root vegetables, peas (small portion).

Fruits: Fresh or fresh stewed, fresh fruit salad, baked apple or pears. Canned fruit in water. Four portions per day.

Miscellaneous: Saccharine and a little crystal fructose or lactose sweetener. Tea, coffee, low-calorie sodas and minerals, salt, pepper, herbs, spices.

Forbidden

Dairy products: Whole milk, including evaporated, condensed, full cream dried. Cream, mock cream, coffee creamers, sour cream, butter, other cheeses, whole egg, egg yolk, ice cream.

Fats: Other margarines, lard, dripping, suet, cooking fat, meat fat, coconut and palm oil.

Meat, poultry, fish: All fatty meats, sausages, luncheon meats, salami, goose, duck, game and high-cholesterol meats and fish.

Soup: Greasy soups and those containing thickening and whole-milk solids.

Cereals, pastries, cookies: All, including cakes, pastries, sweet cookies, Yorkshire pudding. Bread apart from ration.

Vegetables: Starchy vegetables and potatoes apart from ration.

Fruits: Sweetened, canned (in sugar, saccharine or sorbitol), dried.

Miscellaneous: Sugar, glucose, chocolate, cocoa, malted drinks, candy, nuts, jam, marmalade, honey, sauces, salad dressing, mayonnaise.

WORKING OUT PORTIONS

These portion lists can be used by people on special diets. It is important to check with your own doctor and dietitian first to ensure this is in line with their advice.

Bread Exchange List – Useful for slimmers
The food portions listed here provide equivalent energy to one slice of bread, i.e. 70 calories (294 kilojoules).

1 oz bread: white, brown, French and low-starch (=1 large thin slice)

3 oz potato: plain boiled or mashed

3 pieces of crispbread

1½ tablespoons plain breakfast cereal, e.g. individual pack or ½ cup Corn Flakes/Rice Crispies or 1 Shredded Wheat

1½ tablespoons raw rice or ¼ cup boiled rice

1½ tablespoons raw spaghetti or other pasta or ⅓ cup cooked pasta

1½ tablespoons dry breadcrumbs

⅓ cup corn (off the cob)

⅓ cup baked beans

2 tablespoons raw string/black eye/kidney beans or butter beans or lentils

Carbohydrate Portions – For people on carbohydrate-restricted diets (*see* Introduction, page 10).

Each one of you will have your own carbohydrate portion list to use to add variety to your meals. This is a small list of useful items which will help you to use the recipes in this book.

Food fried in breadcrumbs or batter (if batter is eaten)	=10 g C
4 tablespoons white sauce or thick gravy	=10 g C
2 tablespoons thickening, i.e. flour, cornstarch, breadcrumbs	=20 g C
1½ tablespoons skim milk powder	=10 g C
1 cup liquid skim milk	=10 g C

SUGGESTIONS FOR PLANNING MEALS

These meal plans give a good idea of how to vary meals when using a good-hearted diet. The plan allows for one light meal and one main meal, plus breakfast.

Breakfasts

Cereal, fresh or canned grapefruit, apples, prunes or rhubarb. Fruit juice. Tea or coffee with skim milk. Bread, toast or crispbread, polyunsaturated margarine and marmalade or jelly.

Winter meals

Sunday: Light meal – *baked stuffed pota-
                  toes; apricots in
                  syrup.
               Main meal – roast beef and York-
                  shire pudding,
                  vegetables in season;
                  *apple shortcake.
Monday: Light meal – cottage pie; fresh fruit.
               Main meal – *spiced ham steaks,
                  broccoli and savory
                  rice; *apple mousse.
Tuesday: Light meal – *Cornish pasties,
                  crackers; celery and
                  cottage cheese.
               Main meal – *Spanish cod, carrots,
                  creamed potatoes;
                  *pancakes and
                  orange sauce.
Wednesday: Light meal – *cottage cheese and
                  ham rarebit; fresh
                  fruit.
               Main meal – *Romany chicken,
                  string beans, boiled
                  potatoes; *lemon
                  sherbert.
Thursday: Light meal – savory ground-beef
                  pie; carton of low-fat
                  yogurt with soft
                  brown sugar.
               Main meal – *lemon ginger chops,
                  brussels sprouts,
                  sauté potatoes; *sur-
                  prise meringue.
Friday: Light meal – *Scotch broth and
                  whole wheat bread;
                  fresh fruit.
               Main meal – fried haddock, tomato
                  sauce, peas and
                  French fried pota-
                  toes; *pineapple
                  fluff.
Saturday: Light meal – *cauliflower casserole,
                  whole wheat bread;
                  cottage cheese.
               Main meal – beef stew with
                  dumplings, cabbage,
                  creamed potatoes:
                  *fruit whip.

*Find starred recipes in this book.

Summer meals

Sunday: Light meal – *ham ring mold, green
                  salad, whole wheat
                  bread.
               Main meal – roast chicken, bread
                  sauce, stuffing, roast
                  potatoes, string
                  beans; *summer
                  pudding and *ice
                  cream.
Monday: Light meal – chicken risotto; cottage
                  cheese and crackers.
               Main meal – *paupiettes of plaice,
                  creamed potatoes,
                  peas; rhubarb crum-
                  ble and custard.
Tuesday: Light meal – cottage cheese salad;
                  fresh fruit.
               Main meal – *goulash, braised zuc-
                  chini, new potatoes;
                  *apple or strawberry
                  flan.
Wednesday: Light meal – fish cakes and chips;
                  fresh fruit.
               Main meal – *carbonnade of lamb,
                  string beans, new
                  potatoes; *lemon
                  sherbert.
Thursday: Light meal – *bacon flan; carton of
                  low-fat yogurt.
               Main meal – *deviled chicken, car-
                  rots, savory rice;
                  *fruit salad and
                  *flummery.
Friday: Light meal – cottage cheese and
                  pineapple salad,
                  bread.
               Main meal – *stuffed squash and
                  creamed potatoes;
                  fresh strawberries
                  and *ice cream.
Saturday: Light meal – marinated herrings and
                  salad; whole wheat
                  bread and cottage
                  cheese.
               Main meal – *pork and cider cas-
                  serole, broad beans,
                  new potatoes;
                  *baked bananas and
                  lemon sauce.

Index